MODERN WORLD NATIONS

AFGHANISTAN	IRAN
ARGENTINA	IRAQ
AUSTRALIA	IRELAND
AUSTRIA	ISRAEL
BAHRAIN	ITALY
BERMUDA	JAPAN
BOLIVIA	KAZAKHSTAN
BRAZIL	KENYA
CANADA	KUWAIT
CHINA	MEXICO
COSTA RICA	THE NETHERLANDS
CROATIA	NEW ZEALAND
CUBA	NIGERIA
EGYPT	NORTH KOREA
ENGLAND	NORWAY
ETHIOPIA	PAKISTAN
FRANCE	PERU
REPUBLIC OF GEORGIA	RUSSIA
GERMANY	SAUDI ARABIA
GHANA	SCOTLAND
GUATEMALA	SOUTH AFRICA
ICELAND	SOUTH KOREA
INDIA	UKRAINE

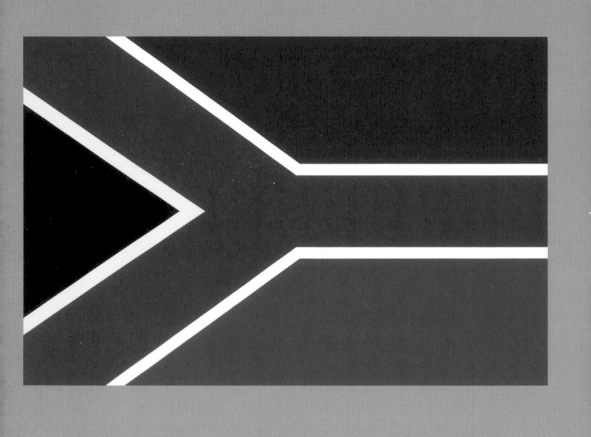

MODERN WORLD NATIONS

South Africa

Vernon Domingo
Bridgewater State College

Series Consulting Editor
Charles F. Gritzner
South Dakota State University

CHELSEA HOUSE
PUBLISHERS
A Haights Cross Communications Company

Frontispiece: Flag of South Africa

Cover: Colorful bathhouses along the coast of South Africa.

CHELSEA HOUSE PUBLISHERS

VP, NEW PRODUCT DEVELOPMENT Sally Cheney
DIRECTOR OF PRODUCTION Kim Shinners
CREATIVE MANAGER Takeshi Takahashi
MANUFACTURING MANAGER Diann Grasse

Staff for SOUTH AFRICA

EXECUTIVE EDITOR Lee Marcott
PRODUCTION ASSISTANT Megan Emery
PICTURE RESEARCHER 21st Century Publishing and Communications, Inc.
SERIES DESIGNER Takeshi Takahashi
COVER DESIGNER Keith Trego
LAYOUT 21st Century Publishing and Communications, Inc.

A Haights Cross Communications ✦ Company

http://www.chelseahouse.com

First Printing

1 3 5 7 9 8 6 4 2

Library of Congress Cataloging-in-Publication Data applied for.

ISBN 0-7910-7610-5

Table of Contents

South Africa

This peaceful view outside Cape Town is much more representative of today's post-apartheid society than that of 50 years ago. With the end of apartheid, the boycotts of South African products have lifted, and products such as wine are now exported for sale in other countries.

1

Introducing
South Africa

South Africa belongs to all who live in it, black and white.

When these words were spoken at a South African outdoor rally in 1955, South Africa was still governed by a racially obsessed government. Population groups were deliberately separated, and certain groups were held to be inferior to others. The policy of *apartheid*—the segregation and domination of all black people by whites—had lasted for more than 350 years. The policy had created poverty, hardship, animosity, and fear. The mostly black crowd that had gathered on that day in the town of Kliptown (Afrikaans for "town of stones"), however, did not show such fear. Instead, they enthusiastically expressed optimism that democracy would someday come to South Africa. Those opening lines of the Freedom Charter of the African National Congress had a parallel in the U.S. Declaration of Independence and its pronouncement that "all men are created free." The goals of these two movements, though separated by two centuries and vast distance, were roughly the same: freedom and democracy.

For South Africans, that day arrived on April 27, 1994, when all South Africans went to the polls to vote, many for the very first time. They were, in fact, creating a democracy by their very action. They had shown that consistent opposition to an evil system could bring about great advances. That steadfast opposition was personified in the life of Mr. Nelson Mandela, a man who sacrificed more than twenty years of his life so that all South Africans could be free from discrimination and oppression. Mr. Mandela, a former political prisoner, had been released from prison in 1990. Four years later he became South Africa's first democratically elected president. This was a truly remarkable feat: A black man was elected to the highest office in a land that had been dominated by whites for more than three centuries. It also personified South Africa's rapid turnaround from an outlaw nation to one that is now eagerly supported by the rest of the world.

APARTHEID: RACIAL DOMINATION

Almost everything that happens today in South Africa takes place against the background of the apartheid years. This is because many of those systems that were put in place have had a lasting influence on events and are slow to change. Even though apartheid—the system of official, legalized discrimination—was overturned in 1994, the effects of 350 years of ill treatment of an 80-percent majority of the population is sure to be apparent for many years and generations to come.

The word *apartheid* has a Dutch origin, meaning "separateness." After the Dutch settled in the southwestern part of South Africa in 1652, they established a colony based on segregation, cheap labor (for some), and slavery (for others). From that time until 1994, South Africa was governed by a minority, non-democratic government with only 14 percent of the population—those classified as "white"—being allowed to vote. This official inequality was very upsetting to many people. It was deeply resented by South Africa's black residents, and also by individuals and many countries throughout the world because of its obvious racist nature.

SOUTH AFRICA IN THE WORLD

The geography of South Africa has ensured that it would become an important player in world events. Its location at the southern tip of Africa was significant for European explorers who, in the fifteenth century, were seeking a sailing route to the treasures of Asia. As they passed the Cape of Good Hope, they would often go ashore for a short refreshment stop to obtain fresh fruit, vegetables, and water. This interest in South Africa's resources would remain a cornerstone of the country's relationship with the rest of the world. When first diamonds and then gold were discovered in the late nineteenth century, South Africa's importance increased drastically throughout much of the world.

Even today, the strategic location of South Africa at the southern tip of Africa is highlighted every time a huge tanker ship passes with its cargo of Middle Eastern oil en route to the United States or Western Europe. During the Cold War, when the United States and the Soviet Union were especially wary of each other, both sides closely watched this waterway. When conflict in the Middle East temporarily closed the Suez Canal, the "South African" passage became even more important.

A STOREHOUSE OF MINERAL RICHES

South Africa has an extraordinarily large share of the world's mineral resources. Except for oil and natural gas, the country has produced many of the basic resource materials that have driven industrial developments in countries throughout much of the world. Minerals such as iron ore, uranium, chrome, cobalt, platinum, and coal are all found in larger quantities in South Africa than in most other countries. Because of its vast mineral wealth, many countries were willing to overlook South Africa's racist policies in order to be assured access to these

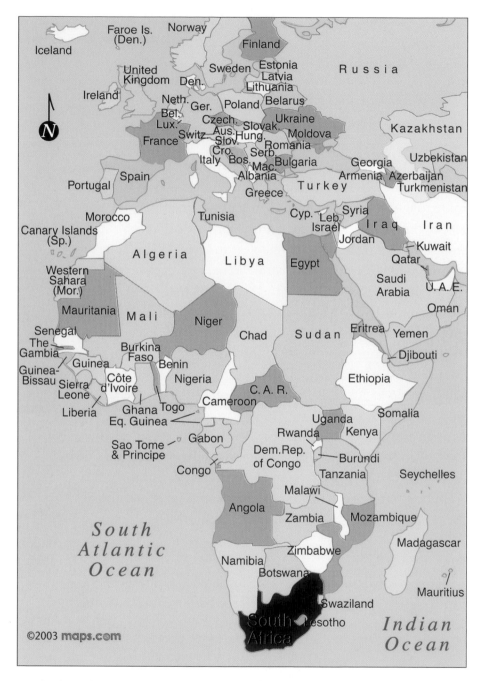

©2003 maps.com

South Africa, located in the southern tip of Africa, has an area of 471,008 square miles (1.2 million square kilometers), which is about twice the size of the state of Texas. Its temperate climate and excellent water access make it a destination for both business and leisure travel.

essential raw materials. However, since the end of apartheid in 1994, many of those countries have tried to make amends for not having supported the long struggle for democracy. One very positive way by which they hope to compensate for past shortcomings is to offer strong support to South Africa's young and fragile democratic government.

A LEADER IN AFRICA

With the end of apartheid and the election of a democratic government, South Africa is set to play a strong role in Africa. It has many internal assets and a high international profile. South Africa's efficient infrastructure—its generally good roads, railway lines, and electricity grid—make it attractive for business investment. Under British colonialism, South African ports were the most highly preferred in all of southern Africa. Many of the railway lines from landlocked Botswana and Zimbabwe were linked to South African ports such as Durban and Port Elizabeth. The result of these physical and economic connections was a region that looked to South Africa for their economic—and later, political—growth. Consequently, South Africa has emerged as the most economically powerful country in Africa that lies south of the equator. It has the largest Gross National Product (GNP) in all of southern Africa. The country also can be a vital part of the efforts to unite the diverse region under a broader umbrella, the Southern African Development Community.

	POPULATION (MILLIONS)	TOTAL GDP (BILLION $U.S.)*	GDP (PER CAPITA)**
South Africa	43.2	113.3	2,622
Zimbabwe	12.8	9.1	711
Botswana	1.7	3.2	1,882
Tanzania	34.4	9.3	270
Zambia	1.7	3.6	2,118

Source: World Bank, 2001
* GDP or Gross Domestic Product is the sum of all goods and services produced within a country in one year.
** Per capita means per person within the country, the total GDP divided by the number of people in the country.

With an economy that is so much larger than that of any other African country, South Africa can play a major role in African (especially southern African) affairs.

SOUTH AFRICA AND THE UNITED STATES

Relationships between the United States and South Africa have focused primarily on social concerns and economic matters. The second of these is the least complex: South Africa has enormous mineral wealth that is needed by the United States. These minerals include gold, diamonds, chrome, and uranium.

It is the social aspect of the relationship that historically has been more complex, troublesome, and yet especially intriguing. Both South Africa and the United States have for a long time been faced with the issues of race and racism. Both countries have been severely divided by these issues. In the United States, for example, more than half a million people lost their lives in the Civil War that was fought at least in part over the issue of slavery. The United States has had major difficulties in fully including black Americans as equal members of society. Even today, blacks have not fully achieved acceptance by and equality within the greater American society. It therefore is not surprising that events in racially divided South Africa have long been compared with the racial struggles in the United States.

In the 1960s and 1970s, when people in South Africa were struggling against apartheid, many of them turned for inspiration to the writings and actions of American figures such as Martin Luther King Jr. and Malcolm X. These individuals were leading larger movements for an end to racial discrimination in the United States, but their loud and clear messages were being heard around the world, and their tactics of opposition to racism were being followed in distant places. In the same manner, the words and actions of South African leaders such as Nelson Mandela and Archbishop Desmond Tutu have had special meaning for Americans still concerned with the struggle against racism and against the vestiges of slavery in the United States.

BLACK AND WHITE LIVING TOGETHER

Beyond its strategic location and great wealth, South Africa has also been a source of insight into how societies can come to terms with each other after a violent past. With the end of apartheid in 1994, South Africans were faced with the prospect of living and working together. To many people, both within South Africa and elsewhere, it seemed like an impossible task. They believed that the memory of so many atrocities of the apartheid era—including the many outspoken opponents to the apartheid system who were jailed or even killed by the South African police and military—would keep flames of hatred burning hotly. The rest of the world has watched in awe as South Africa ended apartheid without the much-anticipated bloodshed. Instead, apartheid was ended through a combination of international economic and sports boycotts, as well as internal political pressure from community groups, churches, students, and trade unions. In the end, negotiations between the last apartheid government and the African National Congress (ANC) led to the release of political prisoners, the "unbanning" of many organizations, and a consensus to have democratic elections.

TRUTH AND RECONCILIATION

With the end of apartheid, South Africans were faced with many important decisions. One of the most delicate problems was what to do about the killings and other atrocities that had taken place under the apartheid government. Its primary objective, after all, was to quiet those voices who called out for democracy and social change. Many opponents of apartheid had been arrested, tortured, and even killed because they had insisted on human rights for all members of South African society. In 1995, the new government established the Truth and Reconciliation Commission. This body was given the task of unearthing the bad deeds of the apartheid era and with providing a forum in which the country could start the healing process. Archbishop Desmond Tutu, a staunch opponent of apartheid and the winner of the Nobel Peace Prize in 1984, chaired the commission. The Commission's primary task was to hear testimony about the acts committed. Members would then decide if amnesty should be granted. It was decided that if misdeeds had been done on behalf of the government, or in an "official" capacity, those responsible should be pardoned.

In heartbreaking session after session, the commission heard testimony from more than 20,000 victims, as well as from many persons who confessed to committing the horrible deeds. By the time it issued its final report in 1998, the commission had granted amnesty in 125 cases. This represents a very small percentage of the more than 7,000 amnesty applications that it had received and reviewed. While the formation of this commission was very controversial inside South Africa, it is generally credited with helping create a more national sense of unity and reconciliation.

Today, South Africa is often seen as a country that has been able to work through its traumatic past and move ahead. Many countries and regions that have had or are facing significant unrest and inter-group hostility have turned to South Africa for inspiration. They are seeking a model that can be adapted to the resolution of their own conflict. While each conflict is unique in terms of its makeup, there are lessons that can be learned from the experiences of others. Conflict-ridden areas of the world, including Northern Ireland and Israel and the Palestinians, have shown a great interest in the strategies developed and used by South Africa.

CONTEMPORARY SOUTH AFRICA

South Africa has undergone more change in the last ten years than many countries have experienced in a century. These changes have had to do with its internal social

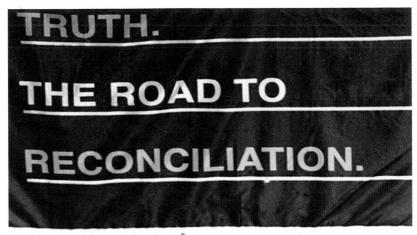

The Truth and Reconciliation Commission had the difficult job of exposing the crimes committed during the apartheid era, and then to hear testimony about the acts committed. Relatives of torture victims as well as those accused testified before the Chairman, Archbishop Desmond Tutu (right), who is seen here handing over the final report to then-President Nelson Mandela on October 29, 1998. In all, only 125 of the more than 7,000 accused were granted amnesty for their actions.

arrangements, as well as with its international relationships. Within the country, there has been a rapid overturning of the old social order. Whites no longer hold all power, authority, and top positions as they did for centuries. Now, in a climate of democracy in which all people are equal in the eyes of the law, we find all South Africans moving— rapidly here, more slowly there—toward a more normal, integrated, and cohesive society.

The former obsession with race has been replaced with a genuine concern for the economic and social development of the long underprivileged members of society. One of the major issues facing South Africa is the continuing high level of inequality that lingers even after the end of apartheid. A typical 14-year-old black girl in a rural South African village still has much less access to adequate food, housing, water, and education than a white girl in the city of Johannesburg. Some black South Africans have benefited from the political changes and have moved into jobs that were previously not available to them. Most of the black population, however, is still trying to catch up with their white counterparts.

The legacy of apartheid will linger for a long time to come. This reality presents many challenges to the new government. Among them, one of the most important is to ensure that programs are available to provide some social and economic safety nets to assist those who may otherwise be left behind in the wake of progress that South Africa is experiencing.

While there are sure to be many difficulties faced by the "rebirth" of this country, it is remarkable that South Africa was able to move beyond the apartheid state without major bloodshed. In this transition to an officially non-racial society, the country has faced many critical challenges and made many landmark decisions. Some people view the changes of the past decades as being a miracle: South

Africa, you will find, is a country of many miracles. It is a beautiful, diverse, and productive land with a rich (though turbulent) history, and a diverse population that looks to the future with great optimism.

South Africa's Cape Town waterfront is a popular tourist attraction. The scenic background view is of Table Mountain, a massive granite landform visible from the Cape of Good Hope. This sight is what originally attracted Dutch colonizers to South Africa.

2

Natural Environment

S outh Africa has long been known for its great physical diversity and striking natural beauty. Early inhabitants such as the San (hunter-gatherers) and the Khoikhoi (cattle farmers) were very appreciative of the wide-open spaces and the availability of a wide variety of food and materials for clothing, tools, weapons, and shelter. Rock art drawn by these groups dates back about 20,000 years and shows a great diversity of wild animals such as eland, and much later domesticated cattle.

These people were self-sufficient and growing in population numbers as they settled into a life of crop and livestock farming. The main grain, called sorghum, and the cattle upon which they depended were introduced into the region by migrants from the north. Both were easily accepted into the social system because the benefits of incorporation were quickly apparent. Both sorghum and cattle were very well adapted to local environmental conditions. Soon, a group arriving by sea would change the physical and political landscape in major ways.

At the end of the fifteenth century, when Dutch colonizers rounded the Cape of Good Hope and saw Table Mountain, a massive granite landform, they were fascinated by the charm of this land. Jan van Riebeeck, writing in his diary, noted that this was "the fairest cape," one teeming with hippos, elephants, and game. The European sailors had discovered a land with abundant fertile soil, adequate moisture, and a nearly year-round growing season. Here, they were able to establish a vital foothold and "halfway station" in a strategic location. A variety of fruits and vegetables could be grown, and water could be obtained to replenish the stock of European ships rounding the Cape en route to the East Indies. South Africa's natural environment was to play a major role in the country's social, economic, and political development.

A TEMPERATE LOCATION

Most of South Africa lies outside the tropics. In fact, 80 percent of the country lies south (poleward in the Southern Hemisphere) of the tropic of Capricorn (23½ degrees south latitude). Its most poleward location, Cape Point at the southern tip of the country, is only 35 degrees south of the Equator. This is comparable to the position of Southern California, which, in fact, shares many similarities with South Africa's physical environment. Because of its middle latitude location, the climate—best described as temperate—is not as oppressively hot as in many other parts of the continent. South Africa also lacks the torrential rainfall and high humidity that characterize the humid tropical portion of Africa.

Because of its climate, South Africa was able to support much larger herds of sheep and cattle. Malaria, sleeping sickness, and many other tropical diseases were never very widespread in South Africa because of its largely cooler, non-tropical conditions. South Africa also attracted many more European settlers than did most of the other African countries. Today, the country's moderate climate—with temperatures that rarely dip very low—help attract tourists. People want to visit a "warm and sunny South Africa" during the northern hemisphere's frigid winter season. The narrowing of the African continent in this region means that the moderating influence of the oceans is very much in evidence. All monthly temperature averages are above freezing. The country also lacks the high or low temperature extremes that are often experienced in locations far removed from large water bodies. Bordering the Indian Ocean, the warm Mozambique Current presents an area where beaches in places such as Durban are especially inviting to tourists. Major international surfing competitions are held annually in South Africa. On the other hand, the cold west-coast waters of the Atlantic Ocean and Benguella Current help make fishing a big part of South Africa's economy.

LAND FEATURES

South Africa's topography (land features), like that of much of Africa, consists of a narrow coastal plain and a large inland plateau with a relatively steep escarpment connecting the two. Much of the inland plateau lies at an elevation between 2,000 and 6,000 feet (610 and 1,830 meters). This interior plateau, which covers nearly two-thirds of South Africa, is at its lowest in the southwest (about 1,000 feet; 305 meters) and it rises towards the north central part of the country, where the city of Johannesburg is located. This northern part of the plateau is called the Highveld (from the Dutch word "field," or characteristic grasses of the high plateau); it lies above 4,000 feet (1,220 meters).

On the Highveld lies perhaps the most important mineral ridge in the world. Here, the Witwatersrand, a rock ridge measuring 62 miles by 23 miles (100 kilometers by 37 kilometers) and with a depth of thousands of feet. This reef contains many valuable mineral deposits. Most importantly, it has been and continues to be the source of most of the world's gold deposits and production. Much of the gold is found at deep levels, beyond 10,000 feet (3,050 meters), making it very hot, difficult, and dangerous work. South Africa has one of the highest rates of mining deaths in the world. After gold was discovered in the Witwatersrand region in 1886, the area grew at an amazingly fast rate. Today the area is the industrial and commercial center of South Africa. Other minerals found in this region include coal, manganese, and uranium.

The Great Escarpment is a spectacular land feature. It is the very steep slope formed as the high interior plateau plunges to the narrow coastal plain. This escarpment reaches its maximum gradient, or incline, in the southeast region where the Drakensberg Mountains form this transition. Here, dramatic peaks reach an elevation of nearly 10,000 feet (3,050 meters) and, on occasion, are even mantled with a cover of snow. The Great Escarpment has made construction of transportation routes from the coast to the interior both difficult and costly. This is particularly true in the southeast, where the escarpment reaches its highest elevations in the Drakensberg range.

In the southern part of the country, inland from an area stretching roughly from Capetown to Port Elizabeth, the escarpment rises sharply to a rough plateau called the Great Karoo and the Little Karoo. The Karoo gets its name from the KhoiKhoi people (Karusa meaning "dry and barren"), and it certainly lives up to its name. It is a semi-desert region, but one with mixed farming, especially in the valleys and where irrigated agriculture can survive.

The coastal plain is a narrow strip of land, rarely more than 10 miles (16 kilometers) wide, that stretches all along the coast of South Africa. On this coastal region are found

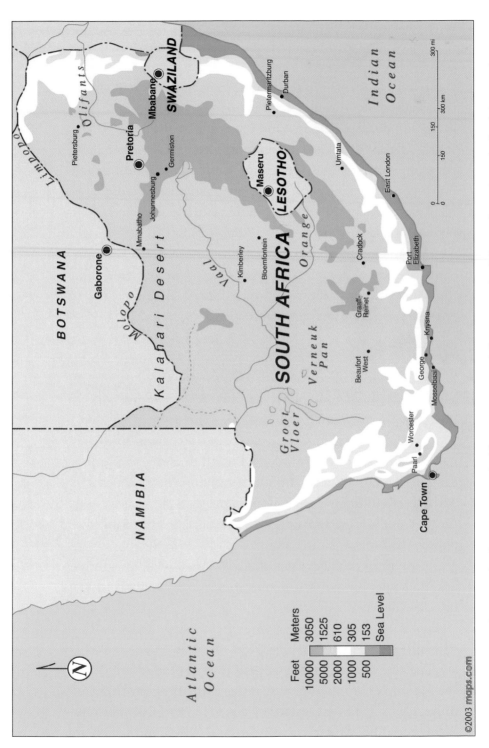

South Africa's towns have a mix of European and African names, partially as a result of the settlers who colonized the country beginning in the seventeenth century. Its rivers are passable by boat only during the rainy season.

numerous cities such as Cape Town, Port Elizabeth, and Durban. The Garden Route is an especially well-known and heavily traveled scenic byway. This scenic corridor links Cape Town and Port Elizabeth, as it winds its way for 500 miles (800 kilometers) through a variety of spectacular landscapes, including coastal lagoons and steep cliffs plunging to the water's edge. (For additional information on this route, including many scenic photographs, enter "garden route south africa" into any search engine and browse the many sites listed.)

A large area of the western coastal plain has very sandy soils because this area was under sea level during the last ice age, about 2 million years ago. In fact, the sea level has fallen by about 300 feet (100 meters), leaving a sandy area referred to as the Sandveld along the southwestern coast. The coastline is fairly smooth and it has few natural harbors.

WEATHER AND CLIMATE

The major feature of South Africa's climate is its lack of rainfall. Many people think of this region—and indeed much of the African continent—as consisting of "jungle." Most of South Africa, however, receives less than 20 inches (50 centimeters) of rainfall. The main reason for the low rainfall is South Africa's latitudinal location (between 22 and 35 degrees south), where a dominant high-pressure system limits cloud formation and precipitation. But it does give South Africa many sunny days!

With ocean on three sides of the country, the temperatures are moderate; the greatest temperature range is found in the interior Highveld region.

Johannesburg, Cape Town, and Durban

The two oceans bordering South Africa, the Atlantic and the Indian, differ in temperature; therefore, they have a direct influence on land temperatures. The cold Benguella Current influences the Atlantic (west) coast, whereas the warm

Mozambique Current keeps temperatures much warmer on the Indian Ocean's (east) coast. This results in significant temperature differences. In comparing temperature averages of Port Nolloth on the west coast and Durban on the east coast, you will note that they lie at roughly the same latitude. However, Durban has an average temperature 10°F (6°C) higher than the west coast. The major economic activities reflect this difference: Durban is a major site for tourists, while Port Nolloth is primarily a fishing port.

The amount and regional distribution of rainfall also has a great impact on South Africa's economic and social changes. About 60 percent of the country receives less than 20 inches (50 centimeters) of rain, making it relatively dry, especially in the interior. Agricultural activity has therefore focused on large-scale, irrigated farming, especially corn (called maize in South Africa) and wheat, which can thrive on low rainfall. In addition, cattle grazing, which involves large tracts of land, has become a major type of land use in the Karoo region. Overgrazing has been and continues to be a major problem in the interior, where far too many cattle and goats graze in a limited area. When such a "carrying capacity" is exceeded, the plant cover is destroyed and often is unable to replenish itself. This has happened in large areas of South Africa, resulting in serious soil erosion and a much lower ability for the land to support grazing or farming activity. Parts of the South African interior are experiencing desertification (creation of desert conditions as a result of human activity). Grasses are depleted and replaced with barren land or useless thorny shrubs.

Where rainfall is higher, in the southwestern region and on the east coast around Durban, different types of agriculture have prospered. Cape Town and its immediate interior have a Mediterranean climate marked by sharp seasonal differences in precipitation. Abundant rainfall occurs during the winter months (May through September), but the summer is extremely dry.

By the eighteenth century, the Bantu peoples were settled cattle and grain farmers living in fixed areas. Cattle were prized possessions, sometimes given with a bride as a dowry.

Because of the lower rates of evaporation in winter, much of the rainfall can be used to grow vegetables and a wide variety of fruits, such as oranges, grapes, and apples. South African fruits are sold overseas, where there is a receptive market. The country has a special competitive advantage because of its Southern Hemisphere location. The reversal of seasons in the respective hemispheres means that South African summer fruits can be produced for Northern Hemisphere markets during their winter season.

In the Durban area, where rainfall is above 40 inches (100 centimeters), tropical fruits such as pineapples and mangoes are grown. The main commercial crop here is sugar, which is grown on the undulating hills west of Durban. In the late 1800s, South Africa, then under British colonial control, brought indentured workers from India, another British colony, to work on the sugar plantations. This has resulted in significant numbers of Indian South Africans now living in the eastern region of the country.

WATER RESOURCES

South Africa has far fewer large rivers than many countries of comparable size. The two main rivers flowing totally within the country—the Orange and the Vaal—arise in the Drakensberg Mountains and then flow westward. Because they originate in a region that receives summer precipitation, their water levels vary a great deal. During the rainy season, their water is deep enough for travel by small boats, but barges cannot travel far on these streams, making them inadequate to play a transport role for agriculture or industry.

During the 1960s, large dams were built on both of the major rivers, thereby taking more water out of the system. The Orange River Project and the more recent Lesotho Highlands Water Project diverted river water to distant agricultural areas, or toward the industrial needs of the greater Johannesburg region.

The Limpopo River rises in the semi-arid neighboring country of Botswana and does not have much water to spare for even dam building. Most of South Africa's rivers are non-perennial—they do not flow throughout the entire year. This, together with the fact that South Africa does not have any significant natural lakes, means that there is a major water shortage in the country. Black South Africans living in the rural areas are hardest hit by this shortage of water. During the apartheid system, they were not included in any plans for water allocation. Today more than half of all black South Africans do not have adequate supplies of water for their domestic needs— drinking, cooking, and washing. Supplying an adequate amount of clean water to its all its people is one of the greatest challenges facing the post-apartheid governments.

NATURAL VEGETATION

Most of the plant life in South Africa, and especially in the drier interior, consists of shrubs and low grasses. Part of the reason for this is that during the nineteenth and twentieth centuries, large areas of land were cleared for crop production and animal grazing. The result has been sparse vegetation that is unable to hold down the already thin soils.

Among the more dramatic-looking trees in the region are the umbrella-shaped acacia and the grotesque, gnarled boabab, both of which provide sustenance to the wild animals in the region. South Africa has only small quantities of commercial trees. Pine forests are found in the southern areas along the Garden Route and in the mountainous regions of the southeast. These commercially valuable species have been introduced into the country from elsewhere.

Much of the timber is used in the mines of Kimberly, the world's major diamond-producing center. Most of the world's gem-quality diamonds originated in South Africa; almost all of the diamonds sold worldwide have had some contact with De Beers, a family-owned South African company that exerts great pressure on the sale and pricing of diamonds everywhere in the world.

ANIMAL LIFE

The savanna region of South Africa is especially well stocked with a variety of wildlife, including elephants, lions, zebras, rhinos, kudu (an antelope), impala, warthogs, and many other species. Successive governments and companies have seen the great economic importance of tourism. Thousands of tourists from many countries flock to South Africa to go on safari (a Swahili word meaning "a journey"). Tourism received its greatest boost with the establishment of the Kruger National Park in 1884. Since South Africa's re-inclusion in the western economies after 1994, many game parks and game reserves have been established, largely for tourists to enjoy seeing the animals

One of the most popular tourist activities is to visit the wildlife game parks and reserves as part of a safari. These trips both boost the economy and preserve the local environment and wildlife, such as these warthogs.

in their natural habitat, rather than in a zoo. South Africa's "Big Five"—lions, elephants, giraffes, zebras, and hippos— are widely advertised to tout ecologically sound ways to preserve the wildlife, while at the same time providing a source of money from tourist revenues.

South Africa is blessed with spectacular scenery, vast mineral wealth, and a generally mild and pleasant climate. It suffers from few natural hazards; drought is the most persistent environmental problem. Lack of adequate water continues to plague many people living in large areas of the country.

Langebaan Beach in Cape Town was the recent site of an exciting discovery: the 117,000-year-old fossilized footprints of what is believed to be a woman.

3

South Africa through Time

S outh Africa has a very long, fascinating, and often turbulent history. In April 2003, an Associated Press release announced that "a human-like fossil skeleton found in South Africa was buried about 4 million years ago, which makes it one of the oldest known hominid discoveries." Whereas the skeleton remains were not those of a "human," they do suggest that the region may have played an important role in the origin of humankind.

A SOUTH AFRICAN EVE—MOTHER OF US ALL?

About 117,000 years ago, a woman walked down to the Langebaan Beach, north of present-day Cape Town, and left her footprints behind. Her footprints set in the wet sand and became fossilized. In 1997, a South African geologist discovered these footprints. They were examined and found to be the earliest trace of a human being ever found anywhere in the world. This link to our distant past has been much discussed. It was at this time—between 100,000 and 150,000 years ago—that the earliest human beings, who were from Africa, began to spread out to other parts of the world. Anthropologists who studied the size of the footprint and the possible weight of the person believe that a woman made the footprint. If this is true, then this woman could be the ancestor of us all.

This would be an appropriate conclusion because South Africa has been the location of many archeological findings that point to its role within Africa as the home of some of the earliest human beings.

THE SAN AND THE KHOI

The footprints and other early remains belonged to the immediate ancestors of groups still living in South Africa. Of all the groups living in the region today, the San and the Khoikhoi—together referred to as the Khoisan—are regarded as having been in South Africa longer than any other peoples. The San (also known as the "Bushmen") live in the interior, drier parts of Southern Africa. (You might recognize these people from a popular motion picture of some time ago, *The Gods Must Be Crazy.*) This area, known as the Kalahari Desert, spans the northern part of South Africa and includes much of neighboring Botswana and Namibia. They are largely hunting and gathering peoples who use bows and arrows to hunt small game. While they do construct temporary shelters from branches and animal skins, the San roam over large areas. This has resulted in their coming into conflict with mining companies that claim the same area.

The Khoikhoi, on the other hand, while related to the San, were originally more settled sheep and goat herders. They lived in the southern coastal part of South Africa, and they were there when Dutch settlers arrived in 1652. The Khoikhoi were willing to barter with the sailors. It soon became clear, however, that the Dutch wanted to seize their land and enslave them. The Khoihkoi resisted, and many were killed in the conflict with the gun-bearing Europeans. One of them, named Autshumato (called "Harry the Hottentot" by the Dutch) collaborated with the colonizers and was despised by his own people. These early meetings between the two cultures produced a mindset that would continue for hundreds of years.

The Khoikhoi were not especially impressed with the Dutch culture (way of life), although they did enjoy the tobacco and alcohol brought by the ships. The Europeans, for their part, viewed the Khoikhoi as un-Christian barbarians. Even though early Dutch observers had spoken positively about many virtues they saw in the Khoikhoi, the natives were severely abused by the colonizers. Disease introduced by the Dutch (sometimes even deliberately!) killed off a large percentage of the Khoikhoi. The Dutch also took many of the Khoikhoi cattle, leaving the native tribesmen in poverty. As a result, the Khoikhoi withdrew into the interior of the region, with many of them turning to hunting and gathering in order to survive. The language and many other aspects of Khoikhoi culture were swallowed by Dutch influences after 1652.

In August 2002, a simple burial in the Eastern Cape of South Africa illustrated how cultures and cultural groups can remain strong and can even be revived after a long period of apparent dormancy. The event that sparked this turnabout for the Khoisan was the return of the remains of Saartje Baartman. This Khoisan woman had been taken forcibly to Europe from South Africa in 1810, where she was paraded as if she were a circus sideshow freak. She died in France, and her stuffed skeleton was displayed in the Museum of Mankind in Paris until 1974. After much negotiation, Ms. Saartje Baartman's remains were returned to South Africa, placed in a coffin draped with the South African flag, and buried with dignity. At the burial ceremony, the chairperson of the National Khoisan Council, Chief Joseph Little said:

> The return of her remains marks the end of almost 200 years of degradation, isolation, and violation of the dignity of Saartje Baartman. It's good to see that the episode has been brought to an end in a dignified manner.

It is widely believed that the discussion surrounding the return of Saartje Baartman's remains could well spur a revival of Khoisan culture. The descendants of the original inhabitants of South Africa may well play a role in future developments in the country.

BANTU SPEAKERS

In parts of eastern and northeastern South Africa, there lived a cattle-herding people who had earlier migrated from central Africa and now occupied the fertile lands of the south. The word Bantu, meaning simply "the people," is a term used to indicate that all the groups spoke languages that had a common ancestry in central Africa. These groups had reached and settled in South Africa by 500 A.D., largely in the eastern and northern part of the country. They were organized into kinship groups (groups of related people) that formed the basis of these societies, with chiefdoms being the basic unit of society.

Most Bantu peoples were settled cattle and grain farmers living in fixed areas. By the eighteenth century they were established as Zulu, Taung, Ndebele, Venda, Xhosa, and several other groups. Some widespread cultural practices included bride-wealth, often in the form of cattle given to the bride's family. Chiefs, as leaders, decided about such matters as the distribution of land and the settlement of arguments within the group. This lifestyle was to change when Europeans extended their claim to territory eastward and invariably came into contact with first the Xhosa, and then other groups.

EUROPEAN COLONIZERS

By 1750 there were about 15,000 Europeans living in the southwestern part of South Africa. They were mostly descendents of Dutch, German, and French settlers, some of whom had fled religious persecution in Europe. Because it was now a Dutch colony in Africa, 8,000 miles away from Amsterdam, they called themselves Afrikaners and they spoke a simplified form of Dutch, called Afrikaans. This language differed in some ways from Dutch in that it included words and phrases obtained from other population groups in that part of Africa, including the Khoikhoi, the Bantu-speaking groups, and Indonesian and Malayan slaves.

The Afrikaners were deeply religious people, belonging mostly to the Protestant Dutch Reformed church. They used the Bible as their primary guide for living. Their interpretation of the Bible convinced them that the races should be kept separate, with white people only in positions of power and authority. This idea of racial separation and domination was to have the greatest negative effect on the country and on its entire population. Considering the Biblical reference to "Love thy neighbor as thy self," these early Dutch settlers certainly interpreted and twisted Christian doctrine to suit their own narrow and bigoted views!

THE COLOUREDS

Even though Afrikaners did not accept mixing of races, the isolation at the southern tip of Africa and the interdependence of the various groups meant that there would be children born from unions between whites and others. Much of this intergroup contact occurred between whites and people who had been brought as slaves from Indonesia and Malaya, areas that were within the Dutch colonial realm. The result of such interracial mixing was the development of a new population group, soon called the coloured people. Coloureds today make up about 9 percent of the total population; while they are still concentrated in the western Cape region (where they are the majority population), they also spread out to the rural areas and to the other South African cities.

EXPANSION OF THE CAPE COLONY

By the end of the eighteenth century, many Afrikaner farmers believed that they needed more land for grazing animals and planting crops. Therefore, they decided to move into other areas of the country. In this eastward movement, they came into contact with Xhosa people who were moving in the opposite direction. The nature of this clash between peoples and cultures was to become the defining feature of South Africa. Both groups were cattle farmers looking for good grazing land, but the Afrikaners were also determined to claim the land for themselves—without any thought of equal inclusion of the Xhosa people. Whereas the earlier Dutch clash with the Khoikhoi was over quickly, the Xhosa proved to a formidable foe.

Among the most celebrated African leaders who led the battle against Afrikaner domination was Shaka, the Zulu chief who led many military campaigns against the colonizers. But eventually the *assegais* (spears) of the local people could not match the guns of the Afrikaners. The frontier zone soon extended across the Great Fish River, which had been regarded as a boundary between the two cultures. The growth of the Cape Colony was also accompanied by those values and social attitudes held by the Afrikaners. These included Christianity, and church missions were set up with local people being converted, often involuntarily. The slave system from the Cape area was also extended, as now Xhosa and other Bantu-speaking groups were forced into slavery.

ARRIVAL OF THE BRITISH

Early in the 1800s, the British occupied and took over the Cape Colony. Their settlement of the Cape was made possible—at least in part—because the power of the Netherlands had been greatly diminished by a series of wars. The Afrikaners were especially upset when, in 1820, a large group of English-speaking settlers landed in Port Elizabeth. The Afrikaners felt that their language was threatened. Slavery also was ended in 1833, under British influence. Feeling culturally defeated, the Dutch decided to leave the southern periphery of the country. Their migration, called the Great Trek, saw more than 5,000 Afrikaners move to the northern interior of South Africa. Here, they established a Boer republic.

GANDHI IN SOUTH AFRICA

After the British annexed the subtropical Natal region in the early 1800s, they started a sugar industry. This plantation economic system required large numbers of low-cost laborers. For this, the British turned to India, another of their colonies. In 1860, the first ship from India arrived in Durban harbor with hundreds of people looking for work in South Africa. They were classified as "indentured workers;" that is, they worked hard for very low wages, and they were expected to return to India after a contract period. These workers were treated very badly: Many were flogged for working too slowly. From the beginning, the East Indians were regarded by the white authorities as being unequal. They were seen as mere units of labor—similar to mules or oxen—whose sole purpose was to do the hard work. One of the limits placed on them was a nine o'clock curfew, and no one was allowed outside after that hour. In many respects, the same forms of racial discrimination practiced against Africans also occurred in the relationship that was established between Europeans and the Asian peoples.

In 1893, a young Indian lawyer named Mohandas Gandhi arrived in South Africa to begin a law practice. He was not especially interested in political issues and was more concerned with earning some money. On a train journey from Durban to Pretoria, an incident changed his whole outlook on life. The trains then, and for the next 100 years, were severely segregated,

Mohandas K. Gandhi (seated, at center) worked tirelessly against apartheid and discrimination after being denied a seat in a "Whites only" section of a train at the end of the nineteenth century. His policy of active nonviolence was still evident in the late twentieth century, when the end of apartheid came about, spurred on by peaceful protests and nonviolent boycotts.

with the best compartments reserved for "Whites only." Gandhi had purchased a first-class ticket, and he insisted on sitting in that compartment. The train conductor refused to listen to any argument, and he physically threw Gandhi off the train. This violent action resulted in Gandhi reexamining his role in South Africa, and he soon became actively involved in attempts to compel the South African government to treat all people with dignity and with equality before the law.

Gandhi stayed in South Africa for the next 21 years, using all his skills to protest against the policies of racial domination. It was in South Africa that he developed his philosophy of active nonviolence (*Satygraha*). This approach opposed injustices by using nonviolent strategies such as labor strikes, consumer boycotts, and marches. Gandhi was jailed many times for leading these protests. By the time he left South Africa and returned to India in 1914, he had left behind a philosophy that would be deeply embedded in South African opposition politics. Soon Gandhi would turn his attention to working for Indian independence from Britain. There he would be known as the Mahatma, meaning the "Great Soul."

During the anti-apartheid protests from 1960 to 1993, Gandhi's heritage was much in evidence. It ensured that the end of apartheid came not through an armed uprising but through many large-scale arrests inside the country, as well as in other countries, including the United States. While an armed overthrow of the apartheid system was threatened, it was Gandhi's philosophy that prevailed. As Gandhi so aptly put it, "An eye for an eye, and soon all of us will be blind."

THE STRUGGLE

Movements against injustices are often given names. In the United States, the eighteenth-century war against the British is referred to as the American Revolution. Martin Luther King Jr., working during the 1960s to get equal rights for black Americans, helped usher in what came to be known as the Civil Rights Movement. In South Africa, the effort to get rid of apartheid was called The Struggle. This reflected an understanding among all oppressed peoples that it would be a long, drawn-out period of defiance that would include marches, workers' strikes,

Summer, 1965: At this public park, the effects of apartheid are as clear-cut as the rules. Black African women sit on the ground, while white men and women occupy the "Whites only" benches. Even though many of the blacks are there looking after white children, during apartheid none would dare sit on a bench.

economic boycotts, and civil disobedience. Most of those who made the biggest sacrifices were black South Africans. They were legally on the bottom of the social, economic, and political ladder and therefore they were the most vulnerable. There were people from the other groups, too—Indian, coloured, and white—who protested and even spent time in jail for their actions. The protestors against apartheid were true to the belief that one has an obligation to oppose an unjust system.

Dennis Brutus was a South African writer who used his poetry and political actions to help bring about change. He had been a high school teacher, and he was arrested and jailed because he wrote and spoke out against apartheid. His writings—and those of many other writers opposing the system of racial segregation—were banned. This meant that a person could be arrested and jailed even for having such writing in his or her possession. In one of his poems, Brutus wrote about Sharpeville, where sixty black South Africans were shot by the police in 1960:

Remember Sharpeville
Remember bullet-in-the-back day
And remember the unquenchable will for freedom.

Brutus was among the many South Africans who were put in prison on Robben Island, near Cape Town. Rather than becoming bitter, he saw a better future:

Somehow we survive
And tenderness, frustrated, does not wither.

A RAINBOW COUNTRY

Since the end of apartheid in 1994, South Africa has proclaimed itself to be a rainbow country. This means that the country consists of many ethnic, racial, and religious groups. The goal is for each group to maintain its traditions (each individual color in the rainbow), but for all groups to be tied together like a rainbow.

Archbishop Desmond Tutu was instrumental in uniting a severely divided nation of people into one where it is no longer considered taboo to cross race lines. He now travels extensively, spreading his message of peaceful tolerance and acceptance.

4

People and Culture

We are a rainbow nation.

With these words, Archbishop Desmond Tutu, a prominent South African, declared that South Africa's 45 million people, divided into many different ethnic groups, had come together in this place to form one nation. During the apartheid years, the different population groups were deliberately kept separate by law. In this way, they did not get to know one another or each other's cultures. Instead of a rainbow nation, South Africa then was a nation of cultural islands—different peoples and ways of life, with little more than residence in southern Africa connecting them.

Since the early 1990s, many dramatic changes have occurred as communications between and among South Africa's different groups of people began to improve. One major change in the way people interacted was the fact that the Immorality Act was removed from the law books in 1985. Under this Act, any intimate social contact across racial lines between men and women was declared illegal. If caught, one could be imprisoned for ten years. By forbidding sexual relationships and marriage between white and "non-white," the government was interfering in the most personal of decisions—with whom one could have a close relationship and marry. Interestingly enough, of course, the nine million South Africans classified as coloured were exactly that—the products of unions between white and non-white.

When the laws were finally changed, people were able to make their own decisions about those with whom they would associate. They now were able to see a South African culture that they could share in common instead of a color line separating people. Marriages and relationships now were able to flourish without thought about breaking the law. This was the most important initial step in the attempt to "de-apartheidize" the society.

DESIGNING A FLAG

One symbol that has come to represent the new South Africa is the new national flag, adopted in 1994. As the date of the first democratic elections crept closer, the government established a commission to develop a new flag. Their task was to develop a symbol that expressed the unification of all South Africans. Schools, community groups, churches, sport clubs, and other groups became involved in this project, sending their suggestions to the committee. Finally, just before the April 1994 elections, the new flag was unveiled. It was immediately embraced and seen as a symbol of a reborn South Africa. The bright flag can now be seen in many different places in South Africa: on T-shirts, hats, key chains, and, of course, proudly flying in appropriate locations. Perhaps the best place to observe the flag is at sports events. There, both black and white South Africans display the flag with a pride that often surprises visitors to the country. It has quickly become a symbol of national unity in country that previously had been very much divided before 1994.

The colors and design of the flag have a significance that makes it so special. Most South Africans give the flag and its details the following meaning:

- **Black:** for black Africa; most South Africans are Black

- **Green:** for the agriculture and food production of the country

- **Yellow:** for the gold wealth of the country

- **Red:** for the blood of those who died trying to make South Africa free

- **Blue:** for the moderate climate with plenty of blue sky

- **White:** for the international symbol of peace and justice, like the white dove

The merging of these colors represents a convergence of the diverse elements that make up South Africa.

The South African flag has already been flown in space, to the delight of many South Africans. In 2002, Mark Shuttleworth, a South African, was aboard a Russian flight and spent some time aboard the international space station. For this, he has been dubbed the first "Afronaut"—the first person from the continent of Africa in space.

CREATING ONE OUT OF MANY

South Africa is very different from many other countries in numerous ways. One important difference is that the county lacks a history of personalities and events that are shared in common. In most other places, there are commonly perceived heroes and valued actions that become part of the national historical lore. In the United States, for example, Abraham Lincoln and Franklin D. Roosevelt tend, for the most part, to generate a widespread sense of national unity. Throughout most of its history, South Africa "heroes" and events were limited in their importance to Dutch, or British, or one (but rarely all) of the native ethnic groups. The new South Africa is still too young to have figures with whom all peoples can identify and take pride. Except for Nelson Mandela and Desmond Tutu, there are no other figures that generate widespread feelings of a common nationhood. Time may yet create a mythology around figures like Albert Luthuli, a leader of the ANC in the 1950s and 1960s; or even F.W. DeKlerk, the last white minority president, who negotiated with Mandela in the changeover. To achieve such broad acceptance, South Africans will need to reexamine the role of earlier patriots. They will have to learn anew, for example, about the work of Sol Plaaatje (1876–1932), a black writer and a campaigner for African rights.

Some reevaluation of earlier history has been occurring since 1994. Before that date, the school textbooks were written from a very biased viewpoint, one that put apartheid and white South Africans in a good light. Educators are now discovering the wealth of interesting people in the black community. In the old apartheid years, the books projected a belief that nothing worthwhile came out of the impoverished black townships.

NATIONAL HOLIDAYS

Most of South Africa's national holidays are new; that is, they were instituted after 1994 in order to create a sense of new national unity. During the apartheid years, the national holidays celebrated only the triumph of white colonizers over the African people. One such example was the December 16 celebration of the Battle of Blood River. This holiday commemorated an 1838 battle in which Afrikaners killed so many Zulus that the Ncome River "ran

April 27 is the most important South African national holiday: Freedom Day. It commemorates the day in 1994 that millions of black South Africans were allowed to vote in an election, and the day that Nelson Mandela, a former political prisoner, was elected president.

red with blood." Black South Africans always resented this celebration of white domination and killing. Since 1994, the date of the former holiday has been retained. Now, however, it celebrates a "Day of Reconciliation," a time to consider the commonalities of the various peoples in South Africa, rather than the domination of one over the other.

Freedom Day, celebrated on April 27, is the most important of all national holidays. It celebrates the importance of the very first day of democracy: April 27, 1994. On that date, millions of South Africans went to the voting polls for the very first time.

The other significant holiday is one commemorating the role of high school students in the elimination of apartheid. June 16 is commemorated each year in memory of the events at schools in 1976. On that date, 700 students were shot and killed by police officers. The unarmed students were peacefully protesting the forced use of Afrikaans as the language of instruction. This day is special in South Africa's history because it caused great outrage by black and white alike, both within and outside of South Africa. Eventually, this anger against apartheid built to such a high level that the government could no longer hold onto power, and an end to its rule was negotiated. On this day, South Africans, along with people in many other parts of the world, remember those students who sacrificed their lives in the defense of freedom.

LANGUAGES

South Africa is different from many other countries in yet another way: Most citizens can speak at least two languages (and many speak more than two). English is widely spoken and understood, largely because of British colonialism. More recently, English has become even more widely known because many South Africans watch television programs such as CNN and MTV. However, South Africa's cultural diversity means that there are many other languages spoken in the country. In fact, the country has eleven official languages that are protected by the constitution: Sepedi, Sesotho, Setswana, SiSwati, Tsivenda, Xitsonga, Afrikaans, English, isiNdebele, isiXhosa, and isiZulu.

THE NATIONAL ANTHEM

South Africa's national anthem is sung at various sporting, educational, and social events. This anthem is a combination of those belonging to the ANC ("Nkosi Sikelela" Africa) and Afrikaners ("Die Stem," or the voice). After some hesitation, this hymn to Africa and to peace has been widely accepted. The anthem may be unique in that it uses four of the country's official languages, plus English. The feeling of Africa-ness is strongly expressed in this beautiful national anthem, coming as it does after so much suffering. The anthem appears below, with the English translation and the various languages labeled.

Nkosi Sikelel iAfrica

Nkosi sikelel' iAfrica	(Lord bless Africa)
Maluphakamis' uphondo Iwayo	(Let its horn be raised)
Yizwa imithanda yethu	(Listen also to our prayers)
Nkosi sikelela,	(Lord bless us,
(*language: isiXhosa*)	
thina lusapho Iwayo	we the family of Africa)
(*language: isiZulu*)	
Morena boloka sechaba sa heso	(Lord bless our nation)
O fedise dintwa le Matswenyeho	(Stop wars and sufferings)
Morena boloka sechaba sa heso	(Lord bless our nation)
O fedise dintwa le Matswenyeho	(Stop wars and sufferings)
O se boloke, O se boloke sechaba sa heso	(Save it, save it, our nation)
Sechaba sa South Afrika - South Afrika	(The South African nation)
(*language: Sesotho*)	
Uit die blou van onse hemel	(From our blue heavens)
Uit die diepte van ons see,	(From the depths of our sea)
Oor ons ewige gebergtes,	(Over our everlasting mountains)
Waar die kranse antwoord gee	(Where the echoing crags resound)
(*language: Afrikaans*)	

Sounds the call to come together
And united we shall stand
Let us live and strive for freedom,
In South Africa, our land.

Perhaps most important about South Africa's new language policy is the fact that for the first time ever, South Africans are learning each other's languages. African languages such as Xhosa and Zulu had never before been widely taught in non-black schools. With the change, white South Africans are now better able to communicate with their black fellow citizens. This is needed to develop a feeling of "Ubuntu" (Zulu and Xhosa word that means "our common humanity," a sense of caring for each other and cooperating). Where language previously separated people, it can now bring them together.

SPORT

In many ways, South Africa is a "sports-crazy" country. With its moderate climate and open spaces, people have long been attracted to sports events. Sport was, of course, segregated. In fact, athletic segregation played a significant role in bringing down apartheid. Under the old order, there was a separation of interests. Blacks were much more interested in sports than were whites, who mostly preferred rugby (related to American football). These distinctions have diminished in recent years as South Africans of all groups increasingly take pride in their national teams.

In June 2002, South Africa's soccer team, nicknamed Bafana Bafana ("The Boys"), played in the Soccer World Cup final series in Japan and Korea. This was only the second time that South Africa had participated in the event. They were cheered by millions of South Africans, black and white alike, and even though they were eliminated in the first round, they returned home to a hero's welcome. This rallying around a sports event brought to mind the action of President Nelson Mandela, who wore a rugby jersey in 1995 to congratulate the national rugby team when it won the Rugby World Cup. This was a very significant event and will long be remembered by South Africans. Coming only one year after the 1994 vote— and with a rugby team that was still largely white—this act of reconciliation between the races was deeply felt.

Sport can be divisive, as it was during the apartheid years when the government made it illegal for interracial groups to compete together—or even against each other. The government prevented foreign teams from entering the country if those

In June of 2002, South African fans waved the national flag in the stands to support their soccer team at the World Cup. Blacks and whites joined together to cheer the team, who were treated to a hero's welcome when they returned to South Africa (despite losing in the first round).

teams contained even one player who was not white. South Africa national teams were chosen only from the white population. Many people opposing apartheid saw sport as an area where pressure could be brought to bear on South Africa. Starting in 1968, South Africa was banned from competing in the Olympic games. This was a major defeat for the white South Africans, who had always been big sports fans. This type of international isolation was a very important part of the widespread inter-national condemnation of apartheid. After Mandela's release from prison in 1990, South Africa was again admitted back into the Olympics and all other international sports bodies.

Sport, and the isolation from sporting competitions, became a valuable tool to tell a bad government that their abusive behavior of their citizens would not be supported. They had to be isolated. This stands out as an example of a nonviolent way in which people in many countries expressed their displeasure with an oppressive government. Today South Africans can play together on the sports field, and people of all races and ethnicities have an opportunity to compete for the honor of representing their country.

MUSIC

Music is one element of culture that South Africans enjoy a great deal. The range of musical styles varies widely, but some in particular stand out. In the expanding interest in world music, the South African group that has most stood out is Ladysmith Black Mambazo, an *a cappella* group (one that sings without instrumental accompaniment). They come from the Kwa-Zulu/Natal province and sing in both English and Zulu. First introduced to a western audience through the efforts of American singer Paul Simon, this group has gone on to assert themselves as major artists in their own right. Many of their lyrics refer to social issues, such as the plight of workers in the South Africa diamond mines and the movement of people from rural areas to the cities.

The music that most South African youth listen to is the local version of hip-hop and R&B, called Kwaito. It is dance music with chanted lyrics, mostly about life in the South Africa townships (ghettos). It is sung mostly in local languages and played in buses, restaurants, and homes. It also includes a fair share of local slang; its popularity is seen as a reaction to the imported brand of hip-hop music. The name itself is derived from the Afrikaans word *kwai*, which in this sense means something "cool," or music with a good vibe. In many ways the popularity of Kwaito reflects a new openness and the freedom to talk openly about conditions in society. Music has always reflected the way in which society is organized; now the freedom of music indicates a society that is practicing its freedom.

The white apartheid government, fearing any uprising, used excessive force during a protest at a school in 1976. The students were objecting to the compulsory use of Afrikaans, a language they considered to be the language of oppression. The deaths and injuries of the students were broadcast worldwide, convincing the world that it was time for a change; this was the beginning of the end for apartheid.

5

Government

If South Africa can change . . .

On Wednesday, June 16, 1976, a tragic event at a high school in Soweto, on the outskirts of Johannesburg, became a source of outrage around the world. The event involving high school students reverberated far beyond South Africa and, in fact, it created a groundswell of support for social and political changes in the way the country was run.

For many weeks, black South African students at the segregated school had been demonstrating against inferior funding of education for blacks. The government was spending approximately eight times as much per student to fund white schools as it was black ones. In addition, the Afrikaner government was insisting that the students be taught in Afrikaans, a tongue that the students regarded as the language of oppression.

The protest march had many students carrying signs with messages such as "Down with Afrikaans." The South African police, fearful of any challenge to the government, appeared at the rally. With no provocation, they started shooting live ammunition into the crowd of students, killing some of them and injuring many others. One student emerged from the chaos, carrying in his arms the body of a 13-year-old schoolmate, Hector Petersen. Hector had been fatally shot; he died before he arrived at an area clinic.

When the photo of Hector was shown in South Africa and around the world, it provoked unprecedented deep anger against the South African government. Many people inside and outside the country believed that there was little chance of reforming the apartheid government. This undemocratic, cruel, and dictatorial government had to be removed and replaced by a more humane system. If a picture can be worth a thousand words, then the picture of the dying Hector Petersen was "a shot heard around the world."

After this tragic event, freedom-loving people around the world stood up to apartheid. They began using a variety of non-violent strategies that eventually would bring down the repressive South African government. These approaches included asking people outside South Africa not to buy South African products such as gold coins, and putting pressure on international companies not to invest their funds in South Africa. In combination, these actions had the result of putting enormous political and economic pressure on the isolated apartheid government. Finally, negotiations were successful in bringing about a change in the way the country was to be governed.

NELSON MANDELA'S LONG WALK TO FREEDOM

Perhaps no other major political figure has had as many rap songs, paintings, and poems written about him (or her) as has Nelson Mandela. Mandela, as nearly all South Africans will agree, is the single most important individual in South

African history. By "reading" his life, one can better see and understand those changes through which South Africa has gained its present status.

Nelson Mandela was born in a rural part of South Africa in 1911. As a youngster, he herded cows for the family and had plenty of time to think about his future. He studied to become a lawyer. Upon completion of his degree, he became one of the one of the first black lawyers to practice in Johannesburg. The 1950s were very difficult times for black South Africans. Starting in 1948, the apartheid government had passed a series of laws that severely discriminated against black people. The government treated black people as inferior and was determined to keep them separate and unequal. Even though Nelson Mandela was well educated and the son of a tribal chief, he was not treated with respect when he had to deal with white people. His Xhosa first name was Rolihlahla, which means "pulling a branch from a tree." In everyday use, the name translates as "troublemaker." This was very prophetic: Mandela would eventually become a major voice of opposition against the increasingly troubled apartheid government.

When Mandela was a university student, he became politically involved and joined the African National Congress (ANC), an organization that was determined to fight the discrimination policies of the white government. Mandela was a very good organizer and an excellent public speaker. In a very short period of time, he became a top official in the organization. In the early 1960s, Mandela was arrested for treason—trying to overthrow the apartheid government. After a trial, he was given a life sentence in a prison for political prisoners on Robben Island, off the coast near Cape Town. At his trial, Mandela made a statement from the dock:

During my lifetime I have dedicated myself to this struggle of the African people. I have fought against white domination, and I have fought against black domination. I have cherished the ideal of a democratic and free society in which all persons live together in harmony and with equal opportunities. It is an ideal which I hope to live for and to achieve. But if needs be, it is an ideal for which I am prepared to die.

These words lived on to inspire the next generation of South Africans as they continued the struggle against apartheid.

Mandela spent 27 years as a political prisoner. He had been arrested not because of any crime committed, only because of his political ideas. In Mandela's case, his political objective was to create a democratic country. Nelson Mandela never lost hope that his dream of a democracy would come true. On February 11, 1990, he was released from prison and allowed back into South African society. The great joy of this event was felt around the world.

Even greater excitement greeted the first democratic South African elections in April 1994, when all people over the age of eighteen—black and white—were allowed to vote. Nelson Mandela was elected president of the country. What an amazing journey it had been: to rise from cowherd, to political prisoner, to the presidency of this formerly deeply divided country! All of this, miraculously, had been brought about with very little accompanying violence. Many people praised this peaceful change. It presented an important example of how bitter conflicts can be settled without bloodshed. In 1993, Mandela and F.W. DeKlerk, the last minority president of South Africa, were awarded the Nobel Peace Prize. These two political rivals stood together to accept the world's highest award for bringing peace to South Africa.

In his autobiography, *Long Walk to Freedom,* Mandela says that he accepted the Nobel Prize on behalf of all South Africans who had fought against apartheid.

Nelson Mandela was a political prisoner in this cell on Robben Island for 27 years. Only four years after his release, he was elected president of South Africa, fulfilling his dream of a peaceful end to the tragic separatist government that had existed for so long.

ELECTIONS OF 1994

On April 27, 1994, the world witnessed a country—which had long suffered under an abusive government—come into the fold of democratic countries. On that day, millions of South Africans, both black and white, stood in lines—often for hours—in order to cast their vote. It was the culmination of one stage of a long battle to get human rights for all South Africans. Also present were official election observers from nearly every country in the world. Their task was to certify that these elections were fair and open, and they did just that.

For black South Africans, this was the very first time that

they had been allowed to vote. At this historic time, an overjoyed Nelson Mandela quoted Martin Luther King Jr.: "Free at last! Free at last!," words that Dr. King had used in his famous 1963 speech in Washington, D.C.

A NEW CONSTITUTION

The eradication of apartheid and the change to a democratic government required major revisions of the South African constitution. The constitution, a written framework that governs a country, is important because it establishes the relationship between people and their government. It can either allow people to participate as equals or limit participation.

Under the apartheid system, the country's constitution had declared that only white South Africans were full citizens. Even though whites represented only 14 percent of the population, the constitution gave them all of the power. This built-in constitutional inequality of the races was one of the first issues that had to be challenged and changed in 1994. After using an interim constitution in 1994, a new constitution was finally adopted in 1996. Since then, this constitution has come to be seen as a standard against which many other systems are measured. It is particularly interesting to note the many similarities between the new South African constitution and that of the United States.

The constitution of South Africa starts out with a clear statement that South Africa is a democratic country in which human dignity, equality, and non-racialism are most important. The U.S. equivalent, although not as wide-ranging, is found in the Declaration of Independence, which states that "all men are created equal." A major difference between the two countries is that the South African Bill of Rights declares that everyone has the right to the following: freedom of assembly, a healthy environment, health care, adequate housing, sufficient food and water, and a basic education. The committee drawing up this constitution in the 1990s believed that it was essential for these rights to be specifically included. South Africa's widespread poverty could not be ignored. As a result, leaders thought that it was important to place these several issues in clear view of the country's conscience in order that they be recognized and addressed.

There are many other differences between South Africa's constitution and that of the United States. Some of these differences reflect the different times and conditions when they were written. Other differences are there because of the different value placed on having a diverse population of different races and ethnic groups. When examining the South African constitution, one is challenged to consider what he or she would want to include in a U.S. constitution were one being written today. What would you include?

Of course, now that the constitution has been written and approved, there comes the difficult task of translating those ideas into action to improve the lives of people.

CHANGES SINCE 1994

One of the most important changes that occurred after 1994 was the dismantling of the "Bantustan" policy. Under this system, the Bantu-speaking black population (about 72 percent of the population in 1970) was forcibly placed in barren "homelands" in the interior of the country. For the most part, black males were, officially and in practice, seen as mere labor units. As a result, they were required to live near the industrial areas, while their wives and children were restricted to the Bantustans. This policy resulted in severe poverty for most black South Africans, as they were forced into these bleak areas that had little hope of becoming economically developed. When apartheid was dismantled, so were the Bantustans.

Elimination of the homeland policy has been of major significance. It means that government policy and force no longer break up family units. The end of apartheid also means that South African blacks are now allowed to move about freely

During apartheid, black South Africans were required to travel with a passbook at all times so that the government could control their movements. These black workers are waiting to apply for new passbooks; in 1960, hundreds of blacks burned their old ones in defiant protest of the treatment of blacks.

within the country. Previously, black South Africans had to carry "passbooks" that severely restricted their movement. If found without a passbook, a person was likely to be arrested, beaten, and jailed.

The apartheid Bantustan policy left a terrible legacy. Huge

numbers of people are now impoverished and still living in desolate rural areas. Most lack adequate income or a level of educational attainment that would facilitate their departure from these remote, underdeveloped areas. The legacy of apartheid still lingers in a large number of very poor rural citizens, most of whom are black. The new government has attempted to improve the conditions in the former homelands through various programs. One strategy has been to focus more of the decision-making at the provincial level. South Africa did not introduce a federal system like that of the United States, where states have significant powers involving taxation and education. Even in South Africa, however, the nine provinces increasingly are being given power to deal with their own social and economic issues.

One outcome of the 1994 changeover—and one that opponents of the new democracy predicted—was the fear of ethnic or "intertribal" war between the various Bantu-speaking groups. This conflict, many believed, would at least partially result from the apartheid government having created divisions within the "non-white" population. The "divide and rule" policy created different levels of discrimination so that the (black) majority would not unite against apartheid, even though it was their common enemy. Fortunately, these dire predictions have not come true, largely because of the ability of national leaders such as Nelson Mandela to appeal to all groups to stay within a united South Africa. As in all societies, tensions do arise between the various groups, but all signs indicate that the new country is strong enough to survive such tests, tests that will without a doubt appear periodically.

INVISIBLE NO MORE

It is important to note that the governmental changes since 1994 have been at both the local and national level. Today, because the majority of South Africa's population is black, the government is composed largely of black representatives.

President Thabo Mbeki (*front left*) is shown here with his wife at a ceremony during the opening of Parliament in Cape Town. The current government is mostly black, more fairly representing its citizens, 75 percent of whom are black.

At the urban level these changes are very dramatic. Most towns and cities now have democratically elected mayors, chosen by the majority of the residents. Most mayors are black because black citizens are treated as equals in voting and in holding office. One strategy during the apartheid years was to include only white areas and white citizens as belonging in the city proper. The black residential areas on the outskirts of the cities were excluded in all deliberations and therefore were not given their fair share of funds for water, electricity, and sewer facilities. In the aftermath of this policy, following the 1994 elections, most official urban (city) populations increased virtually overnight to an average of three times what they had been before. This occurred not because people had suddenly migrated to the city, but because now black South Africans were no longer "invisible." They had been there all the time, but the apartheid policy treated them as being less than human. Finally, the dignity that was denied to black South Africans for 342 years was reclaimed. Today, black South Africans hold major positions of authority in such fields as business, education, and government, and South Africans of all races and ethnicities meet in shopping malls, on sports grounds, and in schools. There is now a much greater chance of these groups getting to know each other and starting to understand what ties them together as citizens of one country.

The astronomical unemployment rate in South Africa has spurred an "informal economic sector"—sidewalks, street corners, and even backyards often double as places of business for a South African who has something to sell or a service to provide.

CHAPTER

6

Economy

South Africa is home to Africa's largest and strongest economy. What happens there economically is important for not only South Africans but also people in many other African countries. South Africa's economic strength rests on a number of factors, including its vast mineral wealth, agricultural productivity, and a variety of interconnected cultural and historical happenings.

Throughout its history, South Africa's economy has been very closely tied to the land and its natural resources. Initially, early hunting and gathering groups gave way to cattle herders, then to grain farmers who relied primarily on maize (corn).

At the dawn of the twenty-first century, there is still a significant dependence on natural resources. Two key discoveries set the course of South Africa's economic history: diamonds in 1867, and gold in 1888. Mining—of diamonds, gold, and other minerals—is by far the most important resource-based industry, and the very foundation upon which the country's economy rests.

In 1867, a young shepherd boy named Klonkie found a shiny stone on the banks of the Orange River. Not knowing what it was, he gave it to one of his friends. When a family member saw it, the shiny object fascinated him, and he tried to cut glass with it. Not yet convinced, he mailed it to a friend, who then confirmed that it was indeed a diamond, one of the most valuable minerals found anywhere. This set off a diamond rush that forever changed South Africa. Before this, South Africa had been a largely agricultural country, content to serve as a halfway station for ships rounding the Cape of Good Hope. Providing these ships with fresh fruit and vegetables was fine for its time, but diamond mining moved South Africa into an entirely different set of economic activities.

The immediate impact of diamond mining was that South Africa received an influx of many more immigrants from Europe. Many of these people were suffering from the social and economic dislocation brought about by the Industrial Revolution and the further rise of commercialism. As hundreds of would-be miners raced to desirable sites, scrambling (often on hands and knees) for diamonds, the social and political system became much more rigid than it had ever been. A color line was firmly laid down: Whites were the only ones allowed to mine the most favored sites.

The discovery of diamonds in 1867 (and gold in 1888) set South Africa firmly on the path to becoming an industrial country. Initially, industry involved little more than producing machinery needed for local mining. Soon, however, other manufacturing industries emerged, and South African manufactured goods began to be exported to other areas of southern Africa. Today, South Africa is the leading industrial country in Africa, producing about one-quarter of Africa's manufactured goods.

South African diamond mines supply about one-half of the world's gem-quality diamonds. Discovered in the late nineteenth century, the diamonds help drive South Africa's economy. When their price on the world market drops, the South African economy becomes sluggish.

MINING

South Africa is often referred to as a "treasure house" of valuable mineral resources. Today, the country produces about 30 percent of the world's gold and about half of the world's gem-quality diamonds. Other mineral exports include coal, manganese, cobalt, and platinum.

South Africa is the world's leading single producer of gold. For the past 100 years, this valuable resource has been the mainstay of the economy. In some years the income from the sale of minerals has provided about 50 percent of the country's total export earnings. Historically, when the demand and resulting price for minerals are high, the country prospers. During recent decades, however, the price for most of the minerals has been dropping. The result has been less income for South Africa and therefore less money available for much-needed development in areas such as education and housing. Gold, for example, has dropped from a high of nearly $700 per fine ounce to below $300. This decline in value, and therefore income, has been very difficult for South Africa. South Africans closely watch the price of gold on the international market on a daily basis. Any drop in the price, which is set in London, means a weakening of the country's economy.

Evidence of the country's weakened economy is evident in the currency exchange rate. During the 1970s, one South African Rand (R1) was equal in value to one U.S. dollar. In 2001, the rate was R1 = $12, causing a great deal of concern in South Africa. Since then, the rate has improved somewhat for South Africa (R1 = $7.2 in April 2003). These fluctuations show the vulnerability of a country for which most imported goods are priced in U.S. dollars. As with the gold price, the international currency exchange rate is followed daily by most South Africans. When the price of gold drops, the amount of money available in South Africa for economic development immediately decreases.

MANUFACTURING

With its wealth of minerals, South Africa has developed a strong manufacturing sector. The availability of abundant coal resources and the presence of rich seams of iron ore and manganese have made it possible for the country to develop an iron and steel industry. Other industries include textiles, machinery, and automobile assembly. While most of these factories are located in the Witwatersrand area, other leading industrial centers are Port Elizabeth and Cape Town. While most of the managerial positions in factories were held by whites under the apartheid system, now many black workers are moving into the better-paying positions, including managerial ones.

Many of South Africa's manufactured goods are exported to other countries, such as the United Kingdom, Germany, and Japan. For those goods not made in South Africa, imports come from the United States, Germany, the United Kingdom, and Japan. Many international companies have branches in South Africa. It is common, for example, to see a Kentucky Fried Chicken sign or a Gap store in South African cities.

CONNECTING THE COUNTRY

The South African economy has been aided by the presence of a well-developed infrastructure. It is blessed with a good system of roads, railway lines, telephone lines, and Internet connections that allow ideas, people, and goods to move easily from one part of the country to another. When the African National Congress discussed a violent overthrow of the apartheid government in the 1960s, the general feeling was that an armed conflict would destroy the infrastructure. With a mostly peaceful transition of power, the roads and railway lines were left intact and ready to move goods within a new, democratic society.

This infrastructure is not only the best developed in the continent, it is also very well maintained. Roads are passable year-round, unlike seasonal roads in some parts of Africa that become unusable during the rainy season. Despite its smooth coastline, South Africa has been able to build good harbors in cities like Cape Town, Port Elizabeth, and Durban; South African goods (as well as products from other southern African countries) can be shipped abroad, and imports from many of the country's trading partners can be received.

South Africa also has more Internet users than any other African country. This is important because much business

While many of South Africa's population still lives in relative poverty, technology nevertheless is making its way through the country. Internet access has boosted commerce, as businesses can more easily attract investors and international trade can be facilitated.

communication takes place on the Internet. In this way, the country has become a competitive place to attract investment.

TRADE UNIONS

The struggle in South Africa during the apartheid years was not just about the right to vote. It also was about improving the quality of life for the general population. It was the workers who led much of the fight against apartheid. These mostly black South Africans were toiling in the mines, factories, and kitchens for very little pay. In addition, they were abused and had no rights to negotiate for better wages. Black trade unions were illegal during most of the apartheid years. In the 1980s, when unions were finally allowed limited rights, they helped bring down apartheid with tactics such as strikes and demonstrations.

Since 1994, workers and the trade unions they have formed have become important contributors to the South African economy. There was finally a recognition that the economy is really about how workers manage to live and produce and sell goods that improve people's lives. The South African constitution acknowledges this reality. It clearly states that everyone has the right to fair labor practices, as well as the right to have trade unions negotiate with factory and mine owners for fair and livable wages. There are separate trade unions for specific areas of economic activity; however, many of these unions have joined together in a large alliance. This organization, called the Congress of South African Trade Unions (or COSATU), is working to ensure that workers share in the progress of the economy. With a total membership of 1.8 million workers, COSATU is bound to be a strong force in future developments in South Africa.

One big area of concern for South African workers, as well as those in many parts of the world, is the issue of privatization. Privatization involves the government sale to private companies of property formerly held public, such as national utilities that control water supplies, electricity, and transportation to private companies. Workers groups are concerned that new private owners will have few restraints and will lay off workers in order for company profits to increase. As long as the government controls these industries, workers have the ability to influence policy by voting their interests. The trade unions are aware that the national constitution does give them the right to strike. In the absence of a national minimum wage, strikes become an important way to get the government and business to pay attention to the living standards of workers.

Concern with jobs and job security is especially high in South Africa, where the unemployment rate is above 40 percent. (Compare this to the United States, where an unemployment rate of 8 percent is considered to be alarmingly high.) Most of the unemployed are black South Africans who are desperate to find a job. The unemployment rate for blacks is 43 percent; for whites it is only 5 percent. Both government and industry are anxious to encourage investment and job creation because unemployment generates very unstable social, economic, and political conditions.

INFORMAL SECTOR

Visitors to South Africa see the informal economic sector in action: people on sidewalks or at traffic intersections selling goods that include newspapers, fruit, and clothing. With the absence of formal jobs (as in a factory or office), many South Africans—about 25 percent of the entire working population—have turned to the informal sector to make a living. They may set up "businesses" that sell goods on the sidewalk, or even in their own backyards (such as a hairdressing salon). The informal sector is an important part of the economy: It provides hundreds of thousands of people with some income, and thereby keeps money flowing through the nation's economy.

Many children work in the informal sector of the economy. Some are as young as ten years of age; they may work 12 hours a day, standing on the side of the road selling goods. Many of the workers have been very creative in addressing the issue of unemployment. Some have set up dressmaking booths and tire repair facilities, using the most basic of tools. Even though the informal sector does not pay taxes to the government, South Africa has recognized the role of the informal sector and has even made efforts to regulate it.

Much of the informal sector is very creative. For many people it is an essential survival strategy made necessary because regular employment is so rare.

COMMERCIAL AGRICULTURE

One of the most promising features of South Africa's future development lies in its agricultural resources. With its moderate climate and areas of good soils, the country has the ability to feed its entire population and even export food to other countries. One major problem, however, is that of land ownership—who owns the land and how that land will be used. Under apartheid, whites claimed huge areas of the best agricultural land. Blacks (even if they had the money) were not allowed to own any of the better land. They were pushed onto the dry, barren, Bantustan areas where few could eke out a living. Even a decade after the end of apartheid, the problem of land inequality still exists. One result is a high rate of malnutrition among blacks, especially in the rural areas.

In the commercial, white-dominated sector, the main crops grown are maize (corn), wheat, sugar, and tobacco. Vast areas on the Highveld are covered with rolling fields of wheat. In the western Cape area, various types of fruit are the main agricultural crop. Grapes, citrus fruit, and apples are grown in the Hex River valley. It is now possible to buy South African dried fruit in Europe and in North America. South African wines are increasingly sold abroad, providing much-needed foreign revenue for the country.

SUBSISTENCE AGRICULTURE

Most rural black South Africans are subsistence farmers; that is, they grow just enough food for their own families without any produce being left over for sale. Sometimes even subsistence farming is not enough to prevent serious hunger in some areas. These farmers grow maize as their staple food—the main part of their diet. Because maize is a starchy food, the diets are often low in protein intake. Cattle are kept and also are used for food, but their numbers are low because they are expensive, with one cow costing about R4,000 ($450). In the villages, there is a constant struggle for survival, and many of the more physically able people still leave to look for work in the cities. Money that is sent back to the villages by family members fortunate enough to find a city job is an important part of maintaining the rural areas.

Land redistribution has become an important economic and political issue, as many blacks demand that they be given better land on which to grow their crops. While most of the best land is in the hands of white South Africans, little economic development is possible in the black rural communities. During the coming years, there will be increasing pressure to change the patterns of land ownership.

ECONOMIC PLANNING

Since the post-apartheid government came into office, one of its main priorities has been economic development. The government has done much of its planning through a program known as GEAR, which stands for Growth, Employment and Redistribution. The goal, similar to that of the apartheid-era governments, is to achieve a level of overall economic growth that will drive other smaller sectors of the economy. Two additional aspects of GEAR, employment and redistribution, are clearly part of a post-apartheid policy, aimed at providing a better quality of life for black South Africans.

In the past, these two issues were not even on the economic planning agenda, but now that South Africa is a democracy, blacks are insisting that political rights translate into economic justice as well. For the first time in the country's history, its government now has to be responsive to the needs of all people. This is essential in a democracy, but it can be difficult at times, especially with so many competing goals.

The overthrow of the apartheid system was not just about racial injustice; it was also about allowing all people to have a decent standard of living. This is the greatest challenge confronting South Africa's governments as they inherit and attempt to eradicate the terrible economic inequalities created by apartheid.

While many in South Africa are wealthy, there are still many living in poverty; sometimes these are side by side. These shacks in a "township"— what would be called a ghetto in the United States—stand in stark contrast to the green fields and more affluent neighborhoods that border them.

Contrasting Standards of Living

South Africa has a particularly striking contrast in the huge economic gap that exists between its rich and its poor. A visitor to South Africa should visit both the high-rise glass buildings with their attractive shopping malls and the poverty-stricken housing areas known as townships. Often these extremes exist almost side by side. Even so, in a real sense they represent two vastly different places within one country.

Some differences may have developed as a result of the society's competitive economy. It was apartheid, however, that was most responsible for the grossly distorted pattern of income and opportunity. The income differences set by apartheid laws were responsible for very large inequalities in standards of living. The author of this book was raised in South Africa, where he was classified as a coloured. This meant that as a high school teacher in South Africa, he earned only

72 percent of what a white teacher earned, and his classes were almost twice as large as those of his white counterparts. In addition, teaching materials and resources were very scarce—often nonexistent. This was the legal policy of the time, not merely practices by different governments.

The result of such inequality has been a very wide gap in levels of economic development between most black and most white South Africans. These disparities do not disappear overnight, as if wished away by a magic wand. They take years—and perhaps decades—of changed policy and allocation of resources to improve the lot of the majority.

Some years after the 1994 demise of apartheid, the legacy of that system can still be seen throughout the country. It is therefore important to know how apartheid functioned, what its impact was, and what the legacy of this segregation is today.

Apartheid operated at three scale levels:

- **The micro-level** refers to the segregation of facilities such as toilets, park benches, buses, and nearly all other facilities.

- **The meso (or middle)-level** involves residential segregation; only certain ethnic groups were allowed to live in particular areas and use its facilities, such as schools, hospitals, and markets.

- **The macro-level** had the Bantustans: the rural, unproductive areas where black South Africans were dumped so that they would lose their South African citizenship.

This apartheid geography meant that people's standard of living was determined by where they were forced to live. Here, population classification and subsequent location determined life chances. These three levels operated for a very long time, and in many ways they became the set way of life for generations of South Africans. The impacts of this discriminatory system are still widely felt today, even though the country is now a democracy.

At the first level of apartheid policy, the micro, it is apparent that many of these practices have changed. Beaches and restaurants that were for a long time restricted to only certain population groups are now open to all. The signs that proclaimed "Whites only" or "Non-whites only" are now gone, found only in museums where the lessons of such racism can be examined. Most of these forms of "petty apartheid" are illegal under the new constitution and are now little more than bitter memories. But some relics remain: One striking place where the rigid segregation will be visible for generations, and perhaps forever, is in the cemeteries. Under the laws of apartheid, people were born in different hospitals, and they were also buried in different (and unequal) cemeteries. Not much can change these cemeteries, and they remain stark reminders of the inequalities of apartheid. The dates on the gravestones quickly indicate a major difference in life expectancy. Black South Africans died, on average, 14 years before their white counterparts.

The second level, the meso—rigid segregation of residential areas—had the deepest and most lasting negative impact on attempts to create a better quality of life for all South Africans. Under apartheid laws, whites not only were paid much more than blacks, they also lived in the better parts of the city. Whites were in much better housing, with amenities such as water, sewage, and electricity. They were closer to the facilities that the city could offer. Blacks, on the other hand, were underpaid and were compelled to live in areas of poverty. These slum areas were overcrowded and did not have adequate water, electricity, and sewage services. Today there are no longer any legal barriers to anyone moving into a particular neighborhood. The last few years, in fact, have seen some black South Africans moving into previously "white only" areas. Still, this problem will not be remedied overnight: The reality for most black South Africans is that they still live in impoverished areas with little access to running water, electricity, or toilet facilities. Attempts at residential integration have moved along slowly, as there are enormous economic differences between white and black. Simply stated, few blacks can afford to buy houses in white areas and pay for the essential residential services.

The macro, or largest, level of the Bantustans has left South Africa with a seriously low level of development in the rural areas. The boundary lines of the old Bantustans were removed in 1994, but many of the people who had been forcibly moved to them years ago still live in these locations. Without money or jobs, it is impossible to make any large-scale resettlement. In rural South Africa, conditions are the worst for black South Africans. Here we find poverty and low levels of economic development.

Now, about a decade after the establishment of democracy in South Africa, there are still grave inequalities in the country. As recently as 2002, President Thabo Mbeki referred to South Africa as "two nations." By this he meant that on the one hand there is a majority of black South Africans who are still poverty-stricken and without jobs, while on the other hand there is the affluent white population. Although they represent only about 13 percent of the population, most whites live comfortable lives. As an index of different levels of well-being, the life expectancy for black South Africans is 58; for Whites it is 72.

While black South Africans make up 75 percent of the population, they earn only 29 percent of the total income. Whites, on the other hand, with only 13 percent of the population, receive about 60 percent of the total income. The visible signs of this racial divide in quality of life are obvious: Within a period of five minutes it is possible to drive on a very good highway that passes a wealthy, largely white residential area and then encounter a vast stretch of shacks that make up a black township. These contrasts are striking and reveal the problems that the country still has to face.

The exceptionally high rate of unemployment has led to a

corresponding high crime rate as people try to find some way to survive financially. The national high crime rate is in itself a problem, because it works to prevent higher rates of investment.

GROWING BLACK MIDDLE CLASS

Despite so much emphasis on black poverty, it also must be noted that there is now a growing black middle class. These are South Africans who for the first time have been able to occupy top positions in industry and business. The Job Reservation Act, a law that prevented blacks from taking the better-paying jobs, has been scrapped. In addition, since the 1990s wages have been normalized, so that for the very first time, blacks and whites earn the same wages for the same jobs. This has meant that some black people have been able to use their education and skills to improve their own income and quality of life.

Members of the growing black middle class now occupy managerial positions in workplaces where, for the first time in South Africa, a black person may be in a position of authority over a white person. In any normal society, it is accepted that education, experience, and merit help move people into a higher economic level, but South Africa is still far from being a normal society. A decade after the establishment of democracy, the presence of a vast, largely black population still suffering from poverty always looms over economic discussions.

Today, there are signs of strain between those blacks who feel left out of the economic growth and those who have achieved some success. On the one hand there is the new middle class; on the other hand there are millions of poor black people who have not seen or experienced any change in their economic position since 1994.

In 2002, there were demonstrations around the country— but they were demonstrations with an ironic twist. These marches saw poorer blacks protesting against wealthier black

South Africans! This type of tension between the classes has never before been significant. Certainly it was not a factor under apartheid, when there were so few black people who could afford middle-class consumer goods. In the years to come, the tensions between poor and middle- or upper-class blacks will certainly be an important issue to watch.

AIDS IN SOUTH AFRICA

No issue in South Africa creates more concern than does AIDS (Acquired Immune Deficiency Syndrome) because the country suffers from one of the world's highest rates of AIDS infection. In 2002, it was reported that about 25 percent of the population was infected with the virus that causes AIDS. This does not mean that all victims are sickly and dying, but it does mean that there are now more people in South Africa living with HIV/AIDS than in any other country in the world. Most of those infected are black South Africans. A disease of such epidemic proportions is already having an impact on the country's social, economic, and political aspects of life. High rates of absenteeism and low productivity are immediate outcomes from such a high infection rate.

A number of reasons have been cited as being the cause of South Africa's excessively high level of HIV/AIDS, including the lack of concern by the outgoing apartheid governments in the early 1990s, the poverty in many areas of the country, and the low levels of education that limit the success of programs aimed at reducing the incidence. One factor that has been highlighted in the last few years has been the reluctance of even a post-apartheid government to tackle the disease. After much delay, the government of President Thabo Mbeki decided in mid-2002 to provide the appropriate medicine to pregnant mothers and newborn babies. This should result in lower rates of infection and hopefully will help reduce this horrible disease.

Education, governmental involvement, and poverty all must be addressed to halt the rapid spread of AIDS in South Africa. This woman has lost three children to AIDS; estimates are that 25 percent of South Africa's population is infected with the virus.

WATER FOR THE POOR

Water is perhaps the single most basic and essential resource: Without water, there is no life. During the apartheid era, the allocation of water to different population groups was not equal. Whites, who held all of the political power, made sure that they had enough water for everyday use, for swimming pools, and to water their lawns. Black South Africans, on the other hand, suffered from a severe lack of water. In 1993, 17 million blacks—more than half of the total black population—did not have access to clean water. There were few taps in homes; most black families had to get their water from a community tap, a well, or the nearest (and almost certainly polluted) river. This meant that there was a very high rate of infection from polluted water supplies.

Since the end of apartheid, more than 10 million black South Africans have gained access to clean water. Still, 7 million people still use polluted water for drinking, cooking, and bathing. In these communities, cholera infections are frequent, and will remain so until new pipes and adequate toilet facilities are provided.

Because the right to clean water is presented as a right in the South Africa constitution, this was made a priority for the government. Since 1994, about 10 million black South Africans have gained access to clean water. This was achieved by extending piped water to black residential areas and by placing taps in houses. This success in South Africa's development was the result of strong political support at all levels of government. The program to ensure that all South Africans have good water supplies is not perfect, but it is one of the country's best success stories since 1994. There are still some 7 million black people who do not have clean water, and the result is the occasional outbreak of cholera, a disease caused by drinking polluted water. More taps and pipes have to be installed, followed by the task of providing proper toilets. These are basic elements of providing a better life for all of South Africa's citizens.

REDRESSING APARTHEID'S WRONGS

Many strategies are being attempted to improve the quality of life for black South Africans. At the government level, these include programs such as providing better water, housing, and electricity. Some other attempts are more controversial, such as programs that try to counter what is seen as the "white privilege" granted by apartheid and by the present-day continuation of some social ideas and practices of the past. Affirmative action programs, which give preference to black job applicants, are seen as one way in which black citizens can get into the economic system. Another idea that has been widely discussed is that of a "white privilege" tax: White South Africans would be taxed at a higher rate, with these taxes going toward providing better schools for blacks. These ideas, though highly debatable, have been raised in South Africa so that thinking can be expanded beyond the present system. The underlying question today plaguing South Africa is whether the current economic system really helps bring about improvements for large numbers of black South Africans, or whether South Africa needs to use more innovative methods.

PROVINCES

Within South Africa there have always been different regions with different physical and cultural environments. When the different regions were pulled together into one country in the eighteenth and nineteenth centuries, the European colonizers were conscious of these differences. They included this knowledge when they devised the regional framework for the country. At one point, the southern Africa region consisted of four different republics. Two—Transvaal and the Orange Free State—"belonged to" the Boers (Afrikaners), and the other two—Cape Colony and Natal—were dominated by the British. In order to keep the units together under one umbrella of a Union, the functions of a capital city were divided into three cities in three different provinces. Cape Town was made the legislative capital, where the laws are made; Pretoria, in the Transvaal province, was declared the executive capital, where the country's president sits; and Bloemfontein, in the Orange Free State, was made the judicial capital, where the Supreme Court holds its sessions. By giving different regions some say in the functions of government, the voters (all white at that time) were able to see their interests served, so they stayed together in the one country.

Today, tensions rise over any discussion of combining the capital functions. It is very expensive to have separate capitals, as government papers have to be moved from Cape Town to Pretoria and back every six months. For the moment at least, South Africa will retain this strange setup of three capitals.

The new provincial structure was itself an attempt to keep the country together. Instead of having all decisions come from central government, the units (like states in the United States) can make some decisions about schools, medical care, and so on. Today, South Africans are just as likely to look to their provincial capital as to the national government for funding. This is becoming more pronounced as the government considers giving more powers to the provinces to levy certain taxes.

The provinces are very different in their physical geography, as well as in their cultural and historical roots. The Western Cape, for example, has always had low numbers of Bantu-speaking groups. After European colonizers effectively destroyed the Khoi and the San people, the population was composed largely of European settlers and slaves imported from Malaya and the Dutch East Indies (Indonesia). The children born of the illegal unions between these two groups later grew to be the largest group. Today, coloureds make up more than 55 percent of the population in this province. In all other provinces, black Bantu-speaking peoples form the majority. As a result of the apartheid policy that gave coloureds more income and freedom than blacks, this province today has close to the highest average income in South Africa.

Guateng Province (the area around Johannesburg) has the country's highest level of income, primarily from gold mining. Most of the other provinces have long suffered under brutal wars of submission won by European settlers, the institution of slavery, and more recently the infamous Bantustan policy. The results can be seen today in the low-income levels in these provinces. Perhaps because of this inhumane treatment, many of the poorest provinces developed strong and uncompromising cultures of resistance to apartheid. It is no accident that many of the heroes of the anti-apartheid struggle were raised in the Eastern Cape province. It was here that the best-known anti-apartheid opponents—Nelson Mandela, Govan Mbeki, Dennis Brutus, and Steve Biko—had their home base. In the midst of this oppression, there arose a major group of fighters in the struggle for black freedom. All of them spent time in political prison, but most survived to see the fruits of their struggle: a democratic and free South Africa.

It is intriguing to note that both Nelson Mandela and the second president of the free South Africa, Thabo Mbeki, came from the Eastern Cape province. A parallel in the United States can be found in Massachusetts, which to date has produced more U.S. presidents than any other state. The state where the American Revolution started (the "shot heard around the world") produced more than its share of national leaders who upheld those principles for which the revolution was fought. In South Africa, so soon after the triumph of democracy, the spirit of stressing those ideals is still very much alive.

While South Africans deeply appreciate the benefits they have gained since the end of apartheid, they now also realize that daily life is not better for all. This festival is commonplace for people living in the cities, but those who live in areas that have not yet received the benefits of equality must not be forgotten as South Africa continues to strive for better living conditions, jobs, and health for all.

Looking toward a Better Future

One decade after the end of apartheid, South Africa is still a society suffering from great inequality. After the excitement accompanying the dismantling of the official apartheid system subsided, South Africans began to realize that much hard work lay ahead if a better society was to be created for all citizens. In South Africa, this task is especially difficult because of the lingering impact that apartheid continues to have on everyday living conditions. Apartheid laws affected every aspect of life, from unequal wages to segregated and unequal hospitals. The conditions could not and have not disappeared immediately, and today they continue to affect South Africans. The celebration of 1994 has passed, and now the country must get on with the difficult and time-consuming task of creating a country in which all people share the resources.

BURDEN OF THE PAST

South Africans have generally been surprised at the very deep impact that apartheid has had on the society. While all societies are shaped by their history, the intrusive nature of apartheid did considerably more to mold the life and character of South Africa and its people. Apartheid was not just a policy, it was a practice that had an impact on virtually every aspect of everyone's life. Under the system's strict segregation policies, apartheid led both black and white South Africans along very different paths of development. Today, almost half of the country's population lives at or below the poverty line. A prompt response and set of reasonable, fair, and effective programs is needed to assure people that the struggle against apartheid will reap some good economic gain for all.

INSTILLING A SENSE OF DIGNITY

One aspect of South African society that has changed enormously is the removal of the veil of indignity that covered non-white South Africans. From 1652 until 1994, fully 86 percent of the population was regarded as inferior. Non-whites had little voice and almost no respect. White references to elderly black people as "boy" and "girl" hurt deeply in a community where high respect is given to one's elders. Apartheid's impact on human relationships meant that a white child could abuse any black adult at any time; often, white parents encouraged such abuse. A daily feature of black South African life was for individuals to be sworn at and even beaten for no real reason other than their race.

Elimination of apartheid and the implementation of democracy have meant freedom from the daily humiliations of the past. There are, of course, situations in which this is not so, but today, when injustices do occur the law is used to prosecute those responsible for discrimination and ill treatment of people. Black South Africans can now "walk tall" and be accepted as full citizens of the country. This emphasis on human dignity and respect is not to be underestimated. Beyond financial security, people everywhere wish only to be treated with respect.

Now for the first time in South Africa's history, friendships and relationships are developing across lines of race and ethnicity. This is an optimistic sign that the future may indeed be multicolored.

THE AFRIKANERS

One group that has had to journey the farthest in changing their role in the country has been the Afrikaners. These white South Africans—descendents of Dutch, German, and French settlers—have long played a major role in the politics of the country. They make up about 8 percent of the total population and speak Afrikaans, a language derived from Dutch that includes words from the local African languages. The Afrikaners lost the Anglo-Boer War (1899–1901) and vowed never to be in a submissive role again. In 1948, they came into power in the white parliament and set up the series of discriminatory laws that would be the bedrock of apartheid.

The last white minority president was Mr. F.W. DeKlerk who, in 1990, released Nelson Mandela from prison and then negotiated with the ANC for what would be a transfer of power. Since 1994, Afrikaners have taken a back seat in political changes in South Africa. Their main religion, the Dutch Reformed Church, has officially apologized for its role in providing a biblical justification for the system. Afrikaners have become marginalized as events pass them by, but as this book went to press in mid-2003, there were rumblings of discontent. Some Afrikaners, unhappy with their position in the new post-apartheid society, have occasionally exploded bombs in black areas, in the hope of destabilizing the government. Thus far, these incidents have been relatively minor, but it remains to be seen to what extent this will affect the running of the country. Some other Afrikaners have insisted on having a separate

"Boerestaat" (the Afrikaans term for a separate political unit for farmers, or Afrikaner country). This idea has been raised many times before, but if Afrikaner discontent grows, it could create a challenge to the notion of South Africa as one undivided country.

THE ANC

The African National Congress (ANC) has long been the main organization working to overthrow apartheid. It was the home base for Nelson Mandela and for most of the country's new leadership. Coincidentally, it was established in 1912, the same year that the National Association for the Advancement of Colored People (NAACP) was founded as one of the leading American civil rights organizations.

It was with the ANC that most negotiations between the apartheid South African government and black interests took place in the early 1990s. The ANC then went on to win more than 60 percent of the votes in the first free and open election in 1994. The then-head of the ANC, Nelson Mandela, became president of the country. In the second election, in 1999, the ANC repeated its showing, and Mr. Thabo Mbeki was appointed president.

Since 1994, the government has not had an easy time satisfying the very high expectations of the people. There are no easy solutions to many of the issues of social and economic development, and poverty is still widespread. However, so far the electorate is still largely loyal to the ANC, and the other political parties have struggled to make inroads. The ANC has achieved something of a mythic standing for its role in defeating apartheid. This happened despite the vicious attacks on the organization by the white minority governments. The government, for example, carried out many assassinations of ANC leaders. Most of these were performed outside the country: The ANC was banned, and as such it was not allowed to operate within South Africa between 1964 to 1990. This also added to the party's special aura.

Today, faced with the many difficulties of running the country, the pressure is mounting on the ANC to perform. Invariably there will be some disillusionment with the ANC, but it is still doubtful whether this will be sufficient to replace it as the majority party in government. The other party waiting in the wings is the Democratic Party, composed largely of whites with some coloured members. As South Africa moves toward a situation of more normalized "politics as usual," the ANC increasingly will be challenged to produce economic results. There will be less talk of the past system, and more on present-day policies and their successes or failures.

FUTURE CHALLENGES

South Africa has astounded many people with its ability to make major changes. Yet great challenges lie ahead, and the country will have to face up to such issues as the high rate of poverty and the high HIV/AIDS rate. These interconnected issues will require firm leadership from all levels of government. Several broader aspects of the economy, such as inflation and the climate for investment, have been stabilized. Much more needs to be done, however, to ensure jobs (or at least a safety net) for the vast pool of poor South Africans. Unless this is done soon, the memory of the anti-apartheid struggle will fade into the distant mists of time, to be replaced by a young generation that is impatient for change and is willing to risk voting the leading political parties out of office. In their place may come organizations such as workers' groups that wish to see more rapid development for all. What is clear now is that whichever way the struggle goes, decisions will be made by the majority of the South African population.

Developments in South Africa may once more call upon the spirit of *ubuntu* that was present in 1994. As noted earlier, *ubuntu* is a Xhosa and a Zulu word meaning "our common humanity," or a sharing of resources. This term appears in government documents and may prove to be an organizing principle for the next stage of South Africa's development. There is a particular Zulu phrase from southern Africa than is important in this regard:

Umuntu ngumuntu ngabantu.

Translated, it says, "a person is only a person through other persons." This notion of South Africans' interdependence and recognition of each other's humanity was the decisive factor in the 1994 success. Belief in this system of thought is once again being called upon in this difficult time of reconstruction. As the complex and often controversial political and economic decisions get debated, South Africans are proud to place the idea of *ubuntu* in the foreground. At the most southern tip of Africa, the 43 million multicultural and multiracial South Africans need a great deal of *ubuntu* and understanding as they face the future together.

Country name	Republic of South Africa
Location	Southern Africa, with Atlantic Ocean on the west and Indian Ocean on the east
Capital cities	Pretoria (executive); Cape Town (legislative); Bloemfontein (judicial)
Other major cities	Johannesburg, Durban, Port Elizabeth
Area	471,008 square miles (1,219,912 square kilometers); about twice the size of Texas
Land features	Narrow coastal plain, steep escarpment, mostly inland; Highveld plateau
Climate	Mostly semi-arid; warm, dry temperate; subtropical moist along the east coast; Mediterranean climate in the southwest
Major water features	Warm Mozambique Current along the east coast; cold Benguella Current along the west coast
Natural hazards	Droughts
Land use	Arable land: 12%
Environmental issues	Degraded soil; water conservation, water allocation, and control measures
Population	43,647,658 (2002)
Population growth rate	1.7% per year
Total fertility rate	2.38 (average number of children born to each woman during childbearing years)
Life expectancy at birth	45
HIV/AIDS prevalence rate	20%
Number of people living with HIV/AIDS	5.2 million
Ethnic groups	Black: 75.2%; White: 13.6%; Coloured: 8.6%; Indian: 2.6%
Religion	Christian: 68%; Muslim: 2%; Hindu: 1.5%; Indigenous and animist beliefs: 28.5%
Languages	English widely spoken; 11 official languages: English, Zulu, Xhosa, Afrikaans, Ndebele, Pedi, Sotho, Swazi, Tsonga, Tswana, and Venda

Facts at a Glance

Literacy	85%
Type of government	Republic
Executive branch	State president
Legislative branch	A bicameral parliament with a national assembly (400 seats) and a council of provinces (90 seats)
Independence	1961: a republic; 1994: a democratic republic
Administrative divisions	9 provinces
Currency	Rand
Labor force by occupation	Services: 45%; agriculture: 30%; industry: 25%
Industries	Mining, automobile assembly, metalworking, machinery, textiles, fertilizer, foodstuff
Primary exports	Gold, diamonds, wool, sugar, fruit
Export partners (*major ones*)	European Union: 33%; U.S.: 20%; Japan: 6%; Mozambique: 2.5%
Imports	Machinery, electrical equipment, computers
Import partners (*primary ones*)	European Union: 41%; U.S.: 11.4%; Saudi Arabia: 7.3%; Japan: 7%

3 million years ago	Evidence of earliest human beings living in the area
15,000 B.C.	Hunter-gatherers live in region; the San in the northern region and the Khoikhoi in the south
300 A.D.	Bantu-speaking people migrated into the area from central Africa
600–1000 A.D.	Large city-states were established in the east and north of present-day South Africa
1488	Barthlomeu Diaz, a Portuguese explorer, rounds the Cape of Good Hope
1600s	Ships from many European countries use the Cape as a refueling station for supplies and as a post office for passing on information
1652	Dutch sailors led by Jan Van Riebeeck land at the Cape and set up a halfway station to provide provisions to passing ships
1657	The Dutch start importing people from Malaya and use them as slaves
1779	Dutch settlers (Boers) migrate eastward; when they come into contact with Xhosa people, they launch commando attacks in order to control the territory and the people
1806	The British capture the Cape
1818	Shaka, a Zulu warrior, leads his people in conquest of parts of the northeastern region
1833	Slavery is abolished in the British colonial territories
1835	The Great Trek commences as 12,000 Boers move eastward, coming into contact with indigenous groups
1867	Discovery of diamonds in the Kimberley region
1888	Discovery of gold in the Witwatersrand region
1894–1914	Mohandas K. Gandhi, an Indian-born lawyer, leads a nonviolent struggle against racially discriminatory policies
1899–1902	Anglo-Boer War; the Boers eventually surrender
1910	The Union of South Africa is established under the Dominion of the British Empire; only whites are allowed to vote
1912	The African National Congress (ANC) is established to fight for rights for black South Africans

History at a Glance

1948 The National Party of the Afrikaners comes to power in the elections; only whites are allowed to vote

1950 The National Party legislates a series of laws centered on the idea of apartheid, keeping the races separate and unequal

1955 At Kliptown on the outskirts of Johannesburg, the ANC organizes a national conference to denounce apartheid and to draw up a "Freedom Charter" that would proclaim a future democratic nondiscriminatory South Africa

1960 Police open fire on anti-apartheid protesters at Sharpeville outside Johannesburg; 69 people are killed, shot mainly in the back

1961 The white minority government declares South Africa to be a Republic, leaving the British commonwealth and ignoring demands for political reform

1962 Nelson Mandela, one of the leaders of the ANC, is sentenced to life imprisonment for plotting to overthrow the South African government

1976 Anti-apartheid rioting breaks out in Soweto, a suburb of Johannesburg; as protests spread throughout the country, police suppression increases; the police kill more than 600 people

1977 Stephen Biko, a leading anti-apartheid activist, is killed by the South African police while in their custody

1990 On February 10, after 27 years as a political prisoner, Nelson Mandela is freed unconditionally

1991–1993 Most apartheid laws scrapped

1994 South Africa's first democratic elections are held; Nelson Mandela becomes president of the country; the ANC receives more than 60 percent of the votes

1996–1998 The Truth and Reconciliation Commission is convened to investigate crimes committed during the apartheid era

1999 South Africa holds its second democratic elections; Nelson Mandela retires, succeeded as head of state by Thabo Mbeki

2002 South Africa hosts the launching of the new African Union, an organization striving to promote cooperation among African countries

Brutus, Dennis. *A Simple Lust: Collected Poems of South African Jail and Exile, including "Letters to Martha."*: London: Heinemann, 1973.

Brutus, Dennis. *Stubborn Hope.* Washington, D.C.: Three Continents Press, 1978.

Christopher, A.J. *The Atlas of Changing South Africa.* London: Routledge, 2001.

Gobodo-Madikizela, Pumla. *A Human Being Died that Night: A South Africa Story of Forgiveness.* Houghton Mifflin, 2002.

Gordon, Sheila. *Waiting for the Rain.* New York: Bantam Doubleday, 1989.

Isadora, Rachel. *A South African Night.* New York: William Morrow & Company, 1998.

Krog, Santjie, and Charlayne Hunter-Gault. *Country of My Skull: Guilt, Sorrow, and the Limits of Forgiveness in the New South Africa.* New York: Crown Publishing, 2000.

Maharaj, Mac (ed.). *Reflections in Prison.* Cape Town: Zebra, 2001.

Mandela, Nelson. *Long Walk to Freedom.* London: Abacus, 1994.

Mda, Zakes. *The Heart of Redness.* New York: Farrar, Straus & Giroux, 2002.

Reader's Digest. *Illustrated History of South Africa.* Cape Town: Reader's Digest Association, 1994.

Sisulu, Elinor. *The Day Gogo Went to Vote.* Boston: Little, Brown and Company, 1996.

Index

Index

Index

Index

About the Author

VERNON DOMINGO is Professor of Geography at Bridgewater State College in Massachusetts where he teaches both physical and human geography classes. He grew up in South Africa where he was classified as "Coloured." In 2002, he was a Fulbright Senior Scholar at the University of Fort Hare in Alice, South Africa. Profesor Domingo is active as a presenter in professional development workshops for teachers. He is one of the state coordinators of the Massachusetts Geography Alliance and is Director of the Southeast Massachusetts Global Education Center.

CHARLES F. ("FRITZ") GRITZNER is Distinguished Professor of Geography at South Dakota University in Brookings. He is now in his fifth decade of college teaching and research. During his career, he has taught more than 60 different courses, spanning the fields of physical, cultural, and regional geography. In addition to his teaching, he enjoys writing, working with teachers, and sharing his love for geography with students. As consulting editor for the MODERN WORLD NATIONS series, he has a wonderful opportunity to combine each of these "hobbies." Fritz has served as both president and executive director of the National Council for Geographic Education and has received the Council's highest honor, the George J. Miller Award for Distinguished Service.